CITY OF

in the Di...

established as the permanent Seat of the Government

—: of the :—

United States

OF AMERICA

taken from actual Survey, as laid out
on the ground.

by R. King

Surveyor of the City of Washington

[1818]

Marine Hospital

EASTERN BRANCH

East Front of the Capitol of the United States
as originally designed by William Thornton and adopted by General Washington, President of the United States.

THE
WHITE HOUSE
AN HISTORIC GUIDE

WHITE HOUSE HISTORICAL ASSOCIATION

with the cooperation of the National Geographic Society

WASHINGTON, D. C.

Distributed by Grosset & Dunlap, New York

Contents

MANUSCRIPT DIVISION, LIBRARY OF CONGRESS

EARLY IMPRESSION *from the original die of the Great Seal of the United States, adopted in 1782. It appears on a commission granted George Washington by the Continental Congress that year.*

Copyright © 1964, by THE WHITE HOUSE HISTORICAL ASSOCIATION, *a nonprofit organization, chartered on November 3, 1961, to enhance understanding, appreciation, and enjoyment of the Executive Mansion. Income from the sale of this book will be used to publish other materials about the White House, as well as for the acquisition of historic furnishings and other objects for the Executive Mansion.*

Text by MRS. JOHN N. PEARCE, *as revised and enlarged by* WILLIAM V. ELDER III *and* JAMES R. KETCHUM.

Photography and production by the National Geographic Society as a public service. Design and production were directed by ROBERT L. BREEDEN, *assisted by* DONALD CRUMP *and* JAMES R. WHITNEY; *photography by* BATES W. LITTLEHALES *and* GEORGE F. MOBLEY, *all of the National Geographic Society staff.*

Administrator and liaison for The White House Historical Association, NASH CASTRO.

FIFTH EDITION

Library of Congress catalog number 62-18058
PRESS OF JUDD & DETWEILER, INC., WASHINGTON, D. C.
COLOR PLATES BY LANMAN ENGRAVING CO., ALEXANDRIA, VIRGINIA
DISTRIBUTED BY GROSSET & DUNLAP, NEW YORK

Introduction

IT IS HEARTENING and reassuring that President and Mrs. Lyndon B. Johnson are giving continuity to the restoration of the White House, which Mrs. John F. Kennedy so admirably began and effectively carried out during her three years of residence there. This is as it should be, for the White House is the most famous house in the United States, symbolizing the character of the highest office in the Republic.

After her husband's inauguration, Mrs. Kennedy decided a series of publications should be prepared to explain every facet of the White House: its history, its architectural significance, its contents. The White House Historical Association was formed to carry out this project. This guidebook is a comprehensive survey of what future publications will deal with in more detail.

The illustrations show the changing appearance of the White House, which has never ceased to be a shrine of American history. Every President except George Washington lived in it, and the great decisions that have determined the destiny of our country have been made within its walls.

Yet the significance of the President's House goes beyond its historical meaning. It suggests a way of life in which we all take pride. We want it to be an example of excellence, with the old and beautiful things which symbolize the dignity of the President's House brought back. We wish to see here as many objects associated with past Presidents as it is possible to recover. This goal can never be completely realized, but the White House will continue to seek this unattainable perfection. It is pleasant to think that this quest has already made new editions of this guide necessary.

These improvements in the White House would be impossible without private donations. And this is right; it is typically American. Elsewhere in the past the great palaces were created by a king or emperor who ordered his painters, sculptors, and cabinetmakers to decorate the building in which he deigned to live. Here the head of the Government welcomes the generosity of private citizens who provide the works of art whose beauty he shares with all his fellow Americans. To everyone who has contributed to this effort we extend our gratitude.

The gifts from private individuals have been as varied as they have been touching. They have ranged from paintings and drawings costing many thousands of dollars to a piece of velvet of exactly the right period, color, and design to cover two chairs which Lincoln once used. The people feel the White House belongs to them. They elect the man fortunate enough to live in it, and he is its guardian on their behalf.

The White House Historical Association has donated substantially of its earnings from the sale of this guidebook to enhance the restoration work. It has made possible the purchase of historic furnishings; the redecoration of several rooms; and the restoration of the East Garden, which President and Mrs. Johnson have designated as the Jacqueline Kennedy Garden.

The guidebook's aim is to make the reader feel keenly his own participation in the life of the President's House. The President hopes that as many Americans as possible will come here and see their heritage and will experience a renewed sense of the wonder and strength of the American tradition. He hopes that foreign visitors who are entertained here will, in these surroundings, sense our Nation's rich and stirring past.

The directors of the White House Historical Association are grateful to those who have gathered, researched, and written the material for this guidebook. They are particularly indebted to the National Geographic Society and to Dr. Melville Bell Grosvenor, the Society's President and Editor. The Society, as a public service, has taken the photographs for the guidebook and supervised its publication.

JOHN WALKER
Director, National Gallery of Art

July 4, 1962

This guidebook is for all of the people who visit the White House each year.

It was planned - at first - for the children. It seemed such a shame that they should have nothing to take away with them, to help sort out the impressions received on an often crowded visit. It was hoped that they would go over the book at home and read more about the Presidents who interested them most. Its purpose was to stimulate their sense of history and their pride in their country.

But as research went on and so many little-known facts were gleaned from forgotten papers, it was decided to make it a book that could be of profit to adults and scholars also.

On the theory that it never hurts a child to read something that may be above his head, and that books written down for children often do not awaken a dormant curiosity, this guidebook took its present form.

I hope our young visitors will vindicate this theory, find pleasure in the book, and know that they were its inspiration.

To their elders, may it remind you that many First Families loved this house - and that each and every one left something of themselves behind in it - as you do now by the effort you have made to come here.

Jacqueline Kennedy

Welcome to the White House!

Some fine old buildings have a life of their own and go on living quite apart from any temporary occupants. I felt this about the White House when, as the wife of a young Congressman, I first visited it. I feel it even more now that my family and I live here for the span of my husband's work.

The White House is not simply the home of the President. Its rooms, its furniture, its paintings, its countless mementos make it a living story of the whole experience of the American people, the habits and the hopes, the triumphs and the troubles and the bedrock faith of our Nation.

As you make your way through the building no doubt many things will speak to you and linger in your memory: in the East Room, the famous painting of George Washington which Dolley Madison took from its frame and removed for safekeeping when the British set fire to the White House in 1814; in the Red Room, the little bronze inkstand inscribed "T. Jefferson, 1804" --think what glorious words flowed from it; in the State Dining Room, the portrait of the musing Abraham Lincoln and carved beneath in the marble mantelpiece the prayer of John Adams that "May none but honest and wise Men ever rule under this roof"; the Diplomatic Reception Room --now so different in appearance --from which Franklin D. Roosevelt, during depression and war, spoke to the Nation in his Fireside Chats.

The President and I are happy that you have come to visit the White House. We are sure you will leave it with heightened interest in the long and stirring heritage which, like the White House itself, belongs to all of us.

Lady Bird Johnson

VICTORY *in its War of Independence brought the need for a permanent Capital to America. Cornwallis's surrender at Yorktown is shown on this antique wallpaper in the President's Dining Room. It has the Hudson River background of the maker's earlier "Scenic America" (page 122).*

The Creation of a Permanent President's House

"ABOUT NOON had ... presented to me by the joint Committee of Congress ...'An Act for Establishing the Temporary and permanent Seat of the Government of the United States.'"

So George Washington, writing in his diary on July 12, 1790, recorded the final decision to move from Federal headquarters in New York City to a permanent city designed for the Capital, in the newly created District of Columbia on land ceded by the States of Maryland and Virginia. While the new city was being built, the Government would reside in Philadelphia until on "the first Monday in December, 1800, the seat of the government of the United States shall, by virtue of this act, be transferred" to a district "not exceeding ten miles square, to be located ... on the river Potomac."

The newly formed Republic had never had a central seat of Government; individual colonies each had their own capitals. The Continental Congress, which brought the new Nation into being and governed it from the voting of independence in 1776 to the creation of the new Government under the Constitution in 1789, had met in various cities in Maryland, New Jersey, and Pennsylvania—chiefly in Philadelphia. In 1784 the Congress accepted New York's offer to provide appropriate quarters.

The old New York City Hall was remodeled into the elegant building renamed Federal Hall (below, left), by the French engineer-architect Pierre Charles L'Enfant, who had earned General Washington's approval when he designed the emblem of the Society of the Cincinnati, the fraternal organization formed by European and American officers of the Continental Army at the close of the Revolutionary War.

New York also began a splendid mansion for the President's House (page 10) but, following the terms of the residence bill, the Government had moved on to Philadelphia before it was completed. In New York, President and Mrs. Washington actually lived in two dwellings: an attractive late 18th-century brick house on Cherry Street (below, right) and, later, in a four-storied

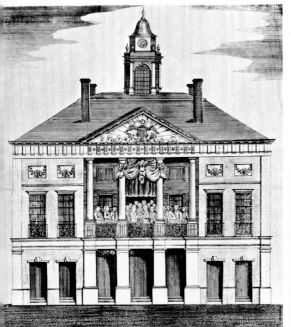

GEORGE WASHINGTON *takes the oath of office as first President of the United States on the balcony of New York's Federal Hall in 1789. While in New York, the Washingtons lived for some time in this house on Cherry Street (below).*

18th-century Broadway residence.

In Philadelphia the first Congress met in the official buildings around Independence Hall, but there was no ready executive residence. The Washingtons lived in a fine house (opposite) rented to them by Robert Morris, "the financier of the Revolution," for whom, it is interesting to note, L'Enfant was then designing and erecting a superb mansion in the French mansarded style. Thus, for the second time, President Washington failed to occupy the planned President's House, the fine brick dwelling with Adamesque detail at left, below. At the end of his second term, in 1797, he retired to Mount Vernon, his Virginia plantation.

Even as the temporary President's House was rising on Ninth Street in Philadelphia, the great project set in motion by the residence bill began: The determination of the location of the Federal District on the Potomac, the laying out of the Capital City, and the designing of the two great Government buildings, the Capitol and the President's House. The story of the selection of the District of Columbia by Washington, Jefferson, and Hamilton is well known, as is the choice of three Commissioners from Maryland and Virginia to supervise the work. In the same period Washington's high regard for L'Enfant prompted him to send the designer to the District to select sites for major buildings. The Georgetown *Weekly Ledger* of March 12, 1791, announced:

> Major Longfont [sic], a French gentlemen, employed by the President of the United States, [has arrived] to survey the lands contiguous to Georgetown where the federal city is to be built.

Undaunted by the rain and snow of the wintry season, L'Enfant explored the area on horseback and frequently transmitted his delight in

LIBRARY OF CONGRESS

THE GOVERNMENT HOUSE in New York, intended as the President's Mansion, was incomplete when the Capital moved to Philadelphia in 1790. This fine Georgian house was eventually used as a customhouse until razed in 1815.

THIS PLANNED PRESIDENT'S HOUSE at Ninth and Market Streets in Philadelphia, with fashionable neoclassic trim, was never occupied by a Chief Executive. The Government moved to the permanent Capital in Washington in 1800.

NEW YORK PUBLIC LIBRARY

ORIGINAL WATER COLOR BY W. L. BRETON, HISTORICAL SOCIETY OF PENNSYLVANIA; MIRROR (BELOW) FROM MOUNT VERNON LADIES' ASSOCIATION

PRESIDENT AND MRS. WASHINGTON *lived, during his term of office, in this house of four bays owned by Robert Morris, at 190 High Street in Philadelphia. While there, they used the Chippendale looking glass (right), probably one of "the two large looking Glasses" owned by the Morrises that Washington noted they "insisted upon leaving."* SECOND FLOOR HALL

GEORGE WASHINGTON *sent this invitation to dine at the Executive Mansion in Philadelphia. Mr. Van Allen was probably of the New York family of this name.*

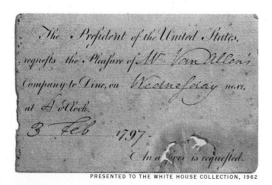

PRESENTED TO THE WHITE HOUSE COLLECTION, 1962

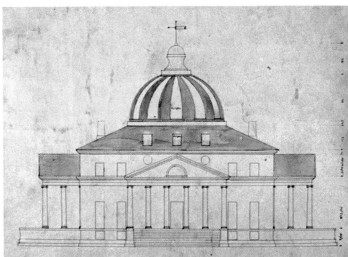

PRIZE-WINNING DESIGN *for the President's House drawn by Irish architect James Hoban. The house, conceived as a Georgian country seat, added an American eagle in the pediment to the more typical features of hipped roof, balustrade, and alternating window arches.*

The upper design at left, based on the Italian Renaissance architect Palladio's Villa Rotonda, was entered by an anonymous "A. Z." Later it was discovered to be the work of Thomas Jefferson.

The lower design was submitted by James Diamond, of Maryland.

NATIONAL PARK SERVICE

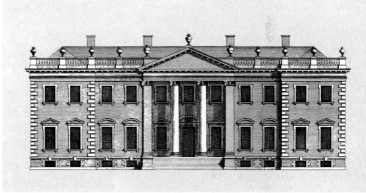

LIBRARY OF CONGRESS

LEINSTER HOUSE, *Dublin, Ireland, above right, is often compared to the President's Mansion.*

TYPICAL DESIGN *from James Gibbs's* Book of Architecture, *the most popular builder's guide of the 18th century.*

CHATEAU DE RASTIGNAC, *in Périgord, France, is also often compared to the President's House. The oval portico is similar to that which Hoban added to the White House in 1824.*

EDITIONS D'ART YVON

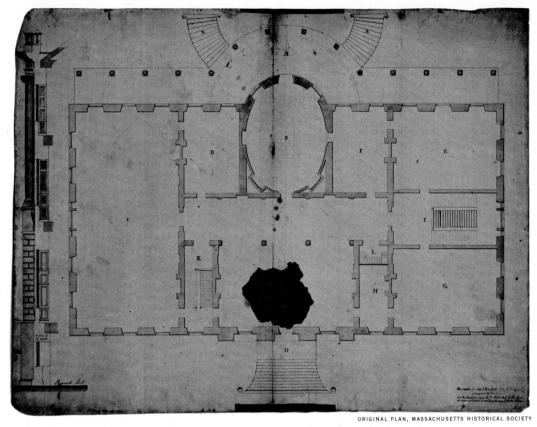

HOBAN'S FLOOR PLAN, *part of his design for the President's House. The elliptical reception room was the most stylish architectural feature of his plan; his proposed Ionic colonnade and portico were not built.*

the noble aspect of the site's hills and rivers in letters to Washington and Jefferson. The most commanding prospect, then known unromantically enough as Jenkins Hill, was described by L'Enfant as "a pedestal waiting for a monument," and he chose it for the Capitol. From this edifice a splendid thoroughfare, Pennsylvania Avenue, was to create a long vista, through which one would see the other great mansion—the President's House—to the northwest.

ARCHITECTURAL historian Fiske Kimball has suggested that the L-shaped relationship of these buildings was based on that of two French royal houses at Versailles: the Palace and the Grand Trianon. L'Enfant's father had been a landscape painter at Versailles, and the young man knew well the great park with its splendid houses and broad avenues. After Pennsylvania Avenue came the other major

avenues and cross streets of his now familiar plan, as shown in the map on the front end papers.

The Commissioners of the Federal City, Thomas Johnson, Daniel Carroll, and David Stuart, established two architectural competitions, one for the design of the Capitol and another for the President's House. In July of 1792 they awarded $500, including a gold medal worth 10 guineas ($46), to James Hoban, an Irish architect then living in Charleston, South Carolina, for his design for the latter (page 12). Among the rejected designs were Thomas Jefferson's adaptation (page 12) of Renaissance architect Palladio's Villa Rotonda, which Jefferson submitted anonymously, and one (page 12) by James Diamond of Somerset County, Maryland, about whose work little is known.

As did the rejected plans, Hoban's design drew in the main on the Palladian architecture of mid-18th-century Europe. This accounts for its similarity to the Château de Rastignac in France (page 13), and to Leinster House in Dublin, Ireland (page 13), to which it is often compared. The general unity of architectural principles in this period is emphasized by these similarities, as well as by the closeness of these houses and many others to the designs in James Gibbs's *Book of Architecture,* published in London in 1728. A typical example from this work, probably the most important architectural design book of the 18th century, is shown on page 13.

The freshness of Hoban's design is only apparent when one examines his floor plan (opposite), which featured as the main drawing room of the house a great oval room (today the Blue Room). The long French doors at the oval end of this room served for many years as the principal access to the mansion from the south, or garden, front.

Work on the President's House, like work on the other buildings of the "Federal City," as George Washington himself modestly referred to it, progressed slowly. But the Government moved as planned in 1800, and our second President, John Adams, supervised the removal of the offices to Washington in June of that year.

On November 1, 1800, President Adams took up residence in the still-unfinished mansion, and on the following evening he included in a letter to his wife, Abigail, the prayer that President Franklin D. Roosevelt had carved on the mantel of the State Dining Room:

"I pray Heaven to bestow the best of

Blessings on this House and all that shall hereafter inhabit it. May none but honest and wise Men ever rule under this roof."

Thus, after nearly three terms of existence of the office of President of the United States, an official residence, though incomplete, was in use. It was the third house begun for the President, and the last; happily, it is still in use today. Abigail Adams's vision that "this House is built for ages to come" is more true with each passing year.

SIGNATURE MARKS OF THE MASONS *who constructed the President's House. The marks, still visible today, were cut into the sandstone above the great fireplace of the old kitchen on the Ground Floor.*

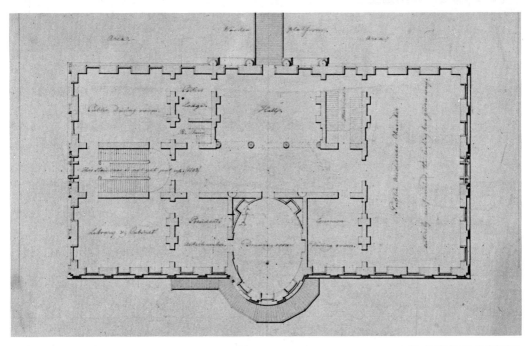

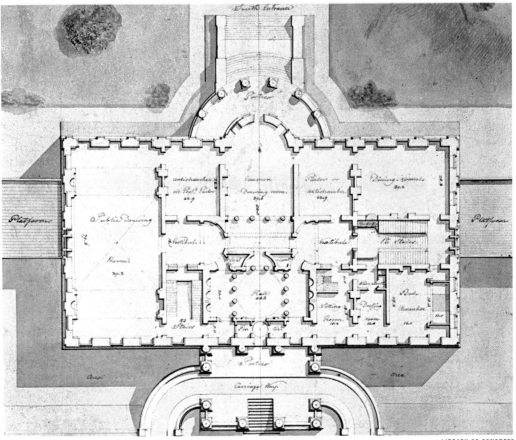

LATROBE MADE THE DRAWING *at top for Jefferson, showing the 1803 floor plan and noting that the main stair was not yet up and the "cieling has given way." In 1807 he proposed embellishments for the State Floor (lower drawing) and the addition of pavilions and north and south porticoes.*

The Changing White House

WHEN the Commissioners for the Federal City chose James Hoban's design for the President's House in 1792, they fully expected the house would be completed when the Government moved to Washington in eight years' time; as we know, it was not. Indeed, it was never completed according to Hoban's original plans. Ever-changing personalities and styles of living and building have inspired the continuing metamorphosis that has marked the history of the White House.

This constant change is symbolized by the development of the wings on either side. L'Enfant had expected that the President's House would have long wings, in the manner of Versailles. Hoban also incorporated wings in his design. This conception was modified, however, by Jefferson and Latrobe, in the low-lying terrace-pavilions which were completed by 1807. Over the years the east terrace was demolished and the west terrace incorporated into the understructure of the Victorian greenhouse.

In the 1902 renovation, a new terrace was built on the east, based on the Latrobe-Jefferson design. The original walls of Jefferson's pavilion on the west were repaired and strengthened and were incorporated into the new terrace. Thus, terraces and other elements of the White House form a living link with the building's past.

These few pages give a brief pictorial survey of some of the changes, and proposed changes, in the White House and its setting. Some are small things, such as the addition of a doghouse next to the southeast gate (page 23). Some are big: Two of the three plans proposed to deal with the unsound condition of the house in 1948 called for its complete demolition. But through the generations the walls of the White House have been strengthened, supported, and enriched from year to year. Perhaps it is most significant that in spite of the many changes, beauty has survived. The White House today is a beautiful house—a symbol of our national heritage, and part of it.

NATIONAL PARK SERVICE

GATEPOSTS TOPPED WITH EAGLES *embellished the approach to the White House from the north in this view of the mansion about 1810. The pavilions built by Latrobe for Jefferson appear on either side of the main house.*

17

THE BLACKENED SHELL OF THE WHITE HOUSE *after the British burned it in 1814, during the War of 1812, is shown in this ominously beautiful engraving by Strickland. Total destruction of the house was prevented only when the fire, still burning against the weakened stone walls, was quenched by a violent thunderstorm that broke on the night of August 24, 1814. Essentially the same walls stand today. On the northeast corner of the roof, what was probably a lightning rod appears bent and twisted by the intense heat.*

BENJAMIN LATROBE'S SENSITIVE DRAWINGS *of the south (upper) and east elevations of the President's House show the exterior changes he proposed to Jefferson. The pavilions and terraces on each side, for which sketches also exist in Jefferson's own hand, were completed in 1807. The North Portico was finished in 1829. The South Portico, completed in 1824, appears to combine Latrobe's design and that of Hoban (page 14). St. John's Church on Lafayette Square, also by Latrobe, appears on the right.*

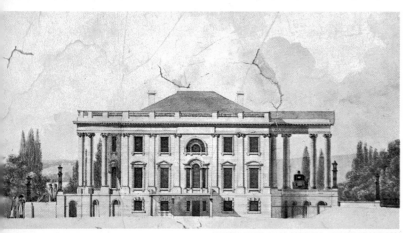

A FRENCH-STYLE *parterre garden appears in front of the South Portico and Jefferson's west pavilion in this English engraving of 1831 by Fenner Sears & Co., after the drawing by Brown. This peaceful arrangement of nature may have been created by Charles Bezat, who was listed in the first Washington city directory (1822) as "gardener to the president."*

ORIGINAL WATER-COLOR DRAWINGS, LIBRARY OF CONGRESS

THE PARKLIKE SOUTH GROUNDS *are shown in this romantic (and inaccurate) view of 1839, after Bartlett. Tiber Creek, in the foreground, then the southern boundary, was filled in the 1880's; Constitution Avenue runs along its course today.*

A PORTICO WITH IONIC COLUMNS *graced the north façade after 1829. The ornamental iron fences were installed in 1833, removed in 1902. The statue of Jefferson, by David d'Angers, now stands in the rotunda of the Capitol.*

OUR
FEDERAL UNION
IT
MUST BE PRESERVED.

ORIGINAL ENGRAVING, LIBRARY OF CONGRESS

DASHING EQUESTRIAN STATUE
of Gen. Andrew Jackson, by
Clark Mills (1810-83), was
erected in Lafayette Square
across Pennsylvania Avenue
from the White House in 1853,
as shown in this handsome
print by T. Sinclairs.
The statue was the first
equestrian bronze cast in
the United States. Mills's
foundry cast Thomas Crawford's
"Statue of Freedom" for
the Capitol dome.

A SMALLER BRONZE VERSION
of Mills's statue, found in
White House storage in 1961,
bears the inscription "Cornelius &
Baker, Philadelphia. Patented,
1855." GROUND FLOOR HALL

WHITE HOUSE COLLECTION © WHITE HOUSE HISTORICAL ASSOCIATION

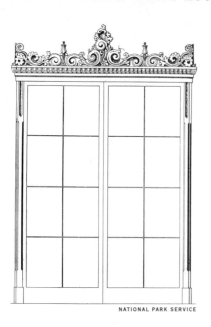

A CAST-IRON VESTIBULE *was among many improvements made in 1853 by Thomas U. Walter, architect of the Capitol wings and dome. A screen of similar design was placed between the columns of the Entrance Hall.*

NATIONAL PARK SERVICE

LANDSCAPE DESIGN *for the President's Park was part of the plan for the grounds between the Capitol and the White House prepared in 1851 by Andrew Jackson Downing, the first great American landscape architect. Downing preserved the simplicity of outline of the White House grounds, but emphasized the English romantic style. Some of his work remains today.*

REDRAWING OF ORIGINAL PLAN, LIBRARY OF CONGRESS

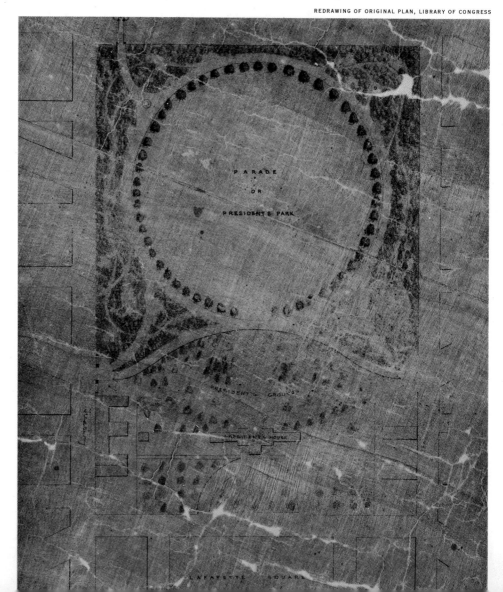

VICTORIAN GATEHOUSE, *dating probably from the 1870's, contrasts with the designs of Downing and Walter, whose work was in some ways the last stage of the classical 19th-century development of the White House.*

IT IS PROBABLE *that a greenhouse existed in the early 19th century, but the first documentary evidence of such construction is dated 1857. In 1867, after a fire, the greenhouses were rebuilt, incorporating into the new structure Jefferson's west pavilion of 1807 (below, center).*

HARRISON ADMINISTRATION'S EXPANSION *plan was the first concrete proposal to enlarge the crowded White House. Under Mrs. Benjamin Harrison's aegis, architect Fred D. Owen executed three designs about 1890. The most extravagant one, of which the south façade is shown here, included large domed wings on either side of the main building and an elaborate new greenhouse. A tour of the entire group would have provided "a promenade of 1,200 feet."*

CLEVELAND'S EXPANSION PLAN OF 1896, *developed during his second administration, also included large wings on either side of the main building. In this case, however, they continued the roof, cornice, and basement lines of the original building, and copied window frames, columns, and other architectural details. In commenting on this design,* Harper's Weekly *noted that the original designers must have had a large winged building in mind; L'Enfant's plan did indeed show long wings.*

NATIONAL PARK SERVICE

McKINLEY'S MODEL FOR AN EXPANDED WHITE HOUSE *was prepared in 1900 under the direction of Col. Theodore A. Bingham, Superintendent of Public Buildings and Grounds. It was a scaled-down version of Mrs. Harrison's plan, with much smaller wings, and stair and cupola details related to the Capitol. The American Institute of Architects condemned it as a monstrosity; the plan was shelved, and the space problem remained unsolved.*

IN THEODORE ROOSEVELT'S ADMINISTRATION, *the White House was finally restored and enlarged by McKim, Mead & White. The main building was left intact, and the Victorian interior gave way to a restrained Classic style. The long-awaited separation of house and office functions was achieved by building on the west side a new Executive Wing, connected to the house by a colonnade, itself part of Jefferson's pavilion (page 19), earlier incorporated into the Victorian conservatory (page 23).*

LIBRARY OF CONGRESS

A FIRE IN 1929 AND RECONSTRUCTION IN 1948-52 *brought about various changes in the White House during the 20th century. The fire occurred in the attic of the Executive Office Wing, requiring President Hoover (watching from the roof at left) to vacate the offices while reconstruction was in progress. Other 20th-century changes include the expansion of the West Wing with the addition of the President's present oval office in 1909; rebuilding of the roof in 1927 to create a new third floor from the old attic; and the building of the East Wing in 1942.*

In the renovation of 1948-1952, the entire interior of the building was removed, and the old wall paneling and other details numbered and stored. A new basement and foundation were built under the original exterior walls, and new steel framework erected inside them. The old paneling and decorative details were reinstalled, and several ground-floor rooms paneled with timbers removed from the interior.

HUGH MILLER, WASHINGTON POST (ABOVE), AND ABBIE ROWE, NATIONAL PARK SERVICE

Life in the White House

AS IMPORTANT as the history of the White House itself is that of the people who have lived there. From the time of the mansion's first occupancy in 1800, the history of the house and of its residents is naturally interwoven. Mrs. Adams, the first wife of a President to live in the Executive Mansion, was horrified at the chilly, unfinished vastness, but consoled herself with the vision of the building's future greatness. She wrote feelingly to her daughter of her dismay, in the frank and ironic manner well-known to readers of her letters:

> The house is upon a grand and superb scale, requiring about thirty servants to attend and keep the apartments in proper order ... an establishment very well proportioned to the President's salary. The lighting the apartments, from the kitchen to parlors and chambers, is a tax indeed; and the fires we are obliged to keep to secure us from daily agues is another very cheering comfort.

Fearing perhaps that she had been too frank, she hastily interposed: "You must keep all this to yourself, and, when asked how I like it, say that I write you the situation is beautiful, which is true." She continued:

> The house is made habitable but there is not a single apartment finished.... We have not the least fence, yard, or other convenience, without, and the great unfinished audience-room [today the East Room] I make a drying-room of, to hang up the clothes in. The principal stairs are not up, and will not be this winter.

It is evident from Abigail Adams's letters that the White House was at first but sparsely furnished, partly with pieces from the President's House in Philadelphia, and partly with the Adamses' own furniture. Thomas Jefferson, upon assuming the Presidency in 1801, made the first serious attempt to complete the building and to furnish it. Finding the house "big enough for two

emperors, one Pope and the grand lama," and still incomplete, Jefferson appointed architect and designer Benjamin Henry Latrobe, Surveyor of Public Buildings, to assist him in carrying out his plans. Latrobe redesigned Hoban's projected South Portico which, when eventually completed in 1824, combined elements of both plans. La-

ABIGAIL ADAMS, *the first President's wife to live in the White House; an original silhouette.*

trobe also designed a North Portico, completed in 1829. The portico not only provided the convenience of a sheltered carriageway, it also dramatically updated the mid-18th-century north façade by the addition of a Classic Revival temple front. Latrobe also constructed for Jefferson pavilions of the sort Jefferson himself designed for Monticello and the University of Virginia. These elegant terraces (page 18) concealed such functional offices as henhouses, laundries, storerooms, and the like. Inside the house, Latrobe made even more up-to-date

GEORGE WASHINGTON, BY GILBERT STUART: *the only object in the President's House since the time of its first occupancy in 1800.* EAST ROOM

ORIGINAL WATER COLOR, LIBRARY OF CONGRESS

MANTELPIECE *and overmantel mirror designed by Latrobe. They are in the Greek Revival style admired by Presidents Jefferson and Madison.*

THE ONLY OBJECT *in the White House today that belonged to our third President, this bronze inkstand with the inscription "T. Jefferson, 1804," was a 1962 gift.* RED ROOM

PRESIDENT MADISON'S *medicine chest was returned in 1939 by a Canadian descendant of the British soldier who carried it off before the 1814 burning.* PRESIDENT'S DINING ROOM

FROM THE NATIONAL ARCHIVES

designs for a variety of mantelpieces in the Greek Revival style (upper left).

Jefferson proved himself the true exponent of the "Revolution of 1800"; his administration was characterized by greater simplicity of manners and the relaxation of the more formal and courtly traditions established by Washington and Adams. Turning from the essentially English tastes of his predecessors, Jefferson imported continental (and particularly French) ideas, furniture, plants, and foods, and established precedents influential for 30 years. Ice cream and macaroni were among the novelties of his frequent dinner parties.

A widower, Jefferson called on his married daughters to preside as hostesses when their family activities allowed, and, during one period of his daughter Martha's residence, her eighth child, James Madison Randolph, was the first infant born in the White House.

On many occasions hostess for President Jefferson, Dolley Madison, as the wife of President James Madison, ushered in a

BUST OF WASHINGTON, *based on Ceracchi's model, is so idealized a likeness that it lost its identity in the late 19th century and was called "the unknown man." It was one of three purchased in 1817.* BLUE ROOM

PRESIDENT MONROE'S SILVER-GILT *flatware, including this knife and serving spoons, was purchased in 1817. Flatware based on this service is in use at the White House today.*

RECENTLY RECOVERED *from storage, this trunk bears a brass plate marked* JAMES MONROE. *It is fitted with compartments to hold large silver pieces and bears the label of a Washington maker.*

LABELED *J. P. Shriner & Co. | No. 609 15th Street | Opposite U. S. Treasury | Fine Trunks and Satchels*

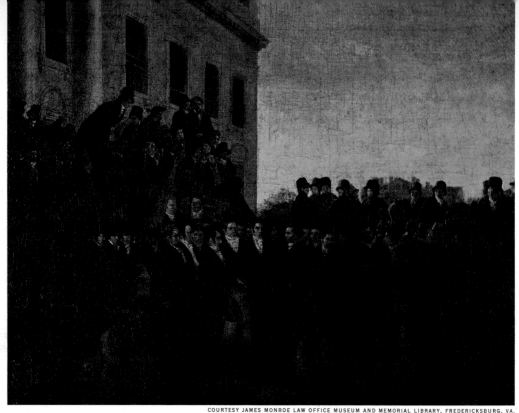

THE EARLIEST KNOWN PAINTING OF THE PRESIDENT'S HOUSE *is this portrayal of the inauguration of President James Monroe in 1817. The north façade of the White House appears in the background.*

MONROE BOUGHT *24 chairs for the East Room from William King, Georgetown cabinetmaker. Only this one is known to exist.*

new era of social life in the White House. Mrs. Madison continued the Jeffersonian tradition of furnishing and maintaining an elegant house. It was at this time that Latrobe's furniture designs (page 106) were executed by Baltimore cabinetmakers John and Hugh Findlay. This furniture, briefly enjoyed by the Madisons, was lost in the fire of 1814.

War with Britain was declared in 1812. As the British drew closer to the Capital during the summer of 1814, President Madison left to support the American troops at the imminent and unfortunate Battle of Bladensburg. Mrs. Madison, alone in the White House, wrote a memorable letter to her sister, reviewing her thoughts and activities. Warned to prepare to leave at a moment's notice, she wrote on August 23, 1814:

... I am accordingly ready; I have pressed as many cabinet papers into trunks as to fill one carriage; our private property must be sacrificed.... I am determined not to go myself until I see Mr. Madison safe, and he can accompany me....

"**THE PRESIDENT'S LEVEE,** *or all Creation going to the White House";*
an unkind caricature of the reception after President Jackson's
inauguration in 1829 is shown in this print by Robert Cruikshank.

On the following day, the day of the burning itself, she wrote again:

> Will you believe it, my sister? We have had a battle, or skirmish near Bladensburg, and I am still here within sound of the cannon! Mr. Madison comes not; may God protect him! Two messengers, covered with dust, come to bid me fly; but I wait for him. . . . At this late hour, a wagon has been procured; I have had it filled with the plate and most valuable portable articles belonging to the house; whether it will reach its destination, the Bank of Maryland . . . events must determine.
>
> Our kind friend, Mr. Carroll, has come to hasten my departure, and is in a very bad humor with me because I insist on waiting until the large picture of Gen. Washington [page 28] is secured, and it requires to be unscrewed from the wall. This process was found too tedious for these perilous moments; I have ordered the frame to be broken, and the canvas taken out; it is done—and the precious portrait placed in the hands of two gentlemen of New York for safe keeping. And now, dear sister, I must leave this house, or the retreating army will make me a prisoner in it, by filling up the road I am direct-

ed to take. When I shall again write to you, or where I shall be tomorrow, I cannot tell!!

This famous portrait by Gilbert Stuart, acquired for the White House in 1800 and the only object from the time of President Adams to survive there, was returned to the rebuilt White House, where it is seen today in the East Room.

The beautiful engraving by Strickland (pages 18-19) is a grim testimony to the condition of the President's House when it was saved from total destruction by a torrential summer storm the night of the 24th. Work was begun under the supervision of the original architect, Hoban, to repair the gutted and roofless mansion.

No vestige of Hoban's interior reconstruction remains today, save for three marble mantelpieces in the fully developed Empire style; two were moved from the old State Dining Room in 1902 to the Red Room and Green Room.

The Madisons did not return, but lived out his term of office in private residences

33

PIECES FROM THE SILVER SERVICE *purchased by President Jackson from the Russian Baron de Tuyll include hot-water pot, coffeepot, cream pitcher, vegetable dish, and wine bucket. Marked by a leading French goldsmith of the early 19th century, Martin Biennais, the silver was purchased in 1833 for $4,308.82.* PRESIDENT'S DINING ROOM

in the city. The Madison administration is today represented at the White House by a small walnut medicine chest that was looted from the mansion by a British soldier at the time of the burning. The chest was returned in 1939 by a Canadian descendant as a gesture of Anglo-American good will (page 30).

President James Monroe, elected to the Presidency in 1816, moved into a rebuilt, but largely unfurnished, White House. Congress appropriated a considerable fund for new furnishings, and Monroe generously offered his own French furniture and silver for the duration of his administration. New furniture and decorative objects were ordered from Paris, and additional purchases were made from cabinetmakers in nearby Georgetown and Baltimore.

A large suite of gilt furniture, of which one piece, a handsome pier table (page 79), has survived in the White House to this day, was made for the Blue Room by the Parisian cabinetmaker Pierre-Antoine Bellangé. Mahogany furniture with ormolu mounts

was ordered for other parlors (page 84), and a splendid group of porcelain and *bronze-doré* (gilt-bronze) ornaments, made by leading craftsmen of the time, graced the tables and mantelpieces.

A silver trunk is the last survivor of six listed throughout the years on White House inventories; they contained the silver and silver-gilt tableware, of which two lovely oval tureens by the French silversmith Fauconnier and a good collection of gilt flatware remain (page 31).

One of Monroe's most important purchases was made in America; three marble busts, of Columbus, Americus Vespucius, and George Washington (page 31), were bought from Benjamin Lear (the son of President Washington's secretary, Tobias Lear) for one hundred dollars each. All are probably by the Italian sculptor Ceracchi and all survive.

With the refurnishing of the President's House, it became again an impressive setting for private and official entertainments. In 1823, John Taylor, a Virginia Senator,

MARBLE BUST *of President Martin Van Buren, by American sculptor Hiram Powers, from the period 1837-1842. It is seen in the portrait of Angelica Van Buren, page 65.* GROUND FLOOR FOYER

SILVER WATER PITCHER *in Empire form is decorated with repoussé flowers and scrolls and is inscribed "Martin Van Buren."* PRESIDENT'S DINING ROOM

noted that "the quality . . . very much resembles that of a private gentleman's furniture. There is only one room spendidly furnished [the Blue Room] . . . designed to impress upon foreign ministers a respect for the Government, which may have a valuable influence upon our foreign relations."

On one occasion during an administration marked by unusual domestic harmony, President Monroe received a delegation of Indian chiefs to whom he presented medals and gifts (page 61). On December 2, 1823, his message to Congress asserted the momentous "Monroe Doctrine," based largely on the diplomatic efforts of Secretary of State John Quincy Adams.

The happy conclusion of Monroe's term was marked by a reception and dinner given for Lafayette on New Year's Day of 1825. "The Marquis," as the Revolutionary War hero was affectionately known to Americans, was making a return visit to the country he had helped to create, a visit that turned into a triumphal tour. The republican spirit of the great French aristocrat is evoked by one of the many airs composed in his honor, displayed in the Red Room.

NO GREAT CHANGES took place in the White House during the administration of John Quincy Adams. Politically and socially, the tide of public opinion was turning to the popular and heroic Andrew Jackson. The inauguration of "Old Hickory" in 1829 was marred by his personal grief at the recent death of his wife. Rachel Jackson had barely survived the great disappointment of her husband's failure to win the Presidency at his first attempt and lived only long enough to share the triumph of his second try. An enormous throng gathered at the inauguration ceremonies to pay homage to "the Hero of New Orleans" and followed him to the crowded reception caricatured by Cruikshank, on page 33.

The two terms of Jackson, "the People's President," were marked by increasing political democracy. The White House, too, saw many changes and improvements. Work began immediately on the North

BLUE-AND-GOLD PORCELAIN BASE
*with bisque kneeling winged figures
supports a gilt fruit or cake basket,
used during the Tyler administration;
it was presented by family descendants.*

MADE *by the firm of E. D. Honoré
of Paris, this plate in rococo-
revival style with United
States' shield and scroll marked
E Pluribus Unum is from the
dinner service used by James
Polk. The plates are decorated
in a variety of colors and flowers,
with gilt touches; here poppies
form the central bouquet.*

VICTORIAN ANDIRONS, *a blend of Chinese
and rococo styles, were used, according to
family records, during the administration of
President Taylor. The andirons were
presented to the White House with
a fender that also had descended
in the Taylor family.* TREATY ROOM

GOLD HEAD *of a walking stick is
inscribed "To the hero of Buena
Vista." Zachary Taylor's part in
the Mexican War brought him
the popularity that aided his
election in 1848.* TREATY ROOM

Portico, which Latrobe had designed in 1807, and Jackson set about furnishing the East Room appropriately for the first time. For this room a bill of $9,358 included, among other items, three cut-glass chandeliers, tables topped with marble, lamps, sconces, vases, curtains, Brussels carpeting, and new upholstery on the 24 armchairs and four sofas of previous administrations.

The descriptions of the balls and dinners given by President Jackson remind one more of Jefferson than any other predecessor. Jessie Benton, daughter of the Senator from Missouri, tells of "the gorgeous supper table shaped like a horseshoe, and covered with every good and glittering thing French skill could devise." A very large and splendid French silver service (of which several pieces are illustrated on page 34) was purchased by President Jackson in 1833 from the Russian minister, Baron de Tuyll. Almost the entire service, made by Martin Biennais, perhaps the best-known Parisian gold- and silversmith of the early 19th century, was recently reassembled from storage areas.

Jackson's table fittings also included an elegant Empire punch bowl, probably the most exciting and elaborate single item in the White House China Collection. Other souvenirs of the Jackson era include the pair of torchères in the Treaty Room (page 138) and the girandole mirror in the Red Room (page 113), possibly one of the President's purchases for the East Room.

It is quite clear that whatever criticism Jackson's "radical" political theories may have received, in matters of taste he followed the fashionable French precedents established by Presidents Jefferson, Madison, and Monroe. In the fine portrait shown on page 107, he is seated in one of President Monroe's Bellangé armchairs.

President Martin Van Buren continued to live in much the same elegant tradition. His political opponents

PRESENTED TO THE WHITE HOUSE COLLECTION, 1962

THIS EMPIRE DESK, *probably purchased during the Jackson administration, was part of 24 wagonloads of furniture sold by President Arthur in 1882.*

IN 1860, *President Buchanan refurnished the Blue Room, unchanged since the Monroe administration. This ottoman, still in the White House, is part of the gilt Victorian set Buchanan purchased from Vollmer and Co. in Philadelphia.* CHINA ROOM

WHITE HOUSE COLLECTION

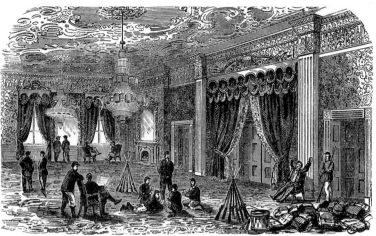

WHITE HOUSE COLLECTION, FROM BENSON J. LOSSING, "PICTORIAL FIELD-BOOK OF THE CIVIL WAR"

TROOPS QUARTERED IN THE EAST ROOM *during the Civil War are shown in this 19th-century wood engraving. The wear and depredation of the room's furnishings at this time necessitated its renovation in 1873 during the Grant administration.*

THE UNION'S CAPITAL, WASHINGTON, *was ironically well situated to watch the grim battle of North and South. Here Northern troops joined the Army of the Potomac, and here the wounded were sent to increasingly crowded hospitals. Lincoln played an active role as Commander in Chief; standing on the North Portico, he reviews a Union battalion. Drawn by F. Cresson Schell, this print was taken from B. P. Poore's* Perley's Reminiscences.

LIBRARY OF CONGRESS

THE RECEPTION OF GEN. ULYSSES S. GRANT *by President and Mrs. Lincoln in the East Room, a painting attributed to Francis B. Carpenter, before the momentous occasion of Grant's appointment as head of the Union Armies. The dignified decor gave way, after the damages of the war, to the increasingly pompous decorations of the late 19th century.*

THE TRAGEDY of Civil War was deepened by the national sorrow at President Lincoln's assassination on April 14, 1865. Here his body lies in state on a black-draped catafalque in the East Room. This engraving, based on a sketch by Alfred Waud, appeared in Harper's Weekly *of May 6, 1865.*

THE OVAL ROOM *on the second floor had been for many years a sitting or reception room, until Mrs. Millard Fillmore made it into the first library in the President's House in 1850. The room is shown here as a library in the Andrew Johnson administration. The settees and center table are still in the White House Collection.*

*"**REB AND BILLY BUTTON** carrying the President's children to school." This sketch by Theodore Davis of President Grant's sons Jesse and Ulysses, Jr., nicknamed Buck, appeared in* Harper's Weekly *of April 17, 1869.*

accused him of aspiring to make the White House "a Palace as splendid as that of the Caesars." Actually, Van Buren made few changes in White House furnishings, confining his activity to repair and refurbishment, including the regilding of the gilt-bronze ornaments purchased in 1817. He is today represented in the White House by a silver water pitcher and the handsome bust signed by the great American sculptor Hiram Powers (page 35).

William Henry Harrison's term ended with his death a month after his inauguration and left no visible impression upon the White House. He was succeeded by his Vice President, John Tyler, whose simple style of country living was transformed by his second marriage in 1844 to the young and beautiful Julia Gardiner, "the Rose of Long Island." The first bride of a President in office, Mrs. Tyler enjoyed her role in the White House and established an extremely regal style. The Tylers are represented in the White House Collection today by a gilt-and-bisque porcelain cake basket, presented by their descendants and located in the Second Floor Hall (page 36).

THE YEARS THAT FOLLOWED were outwardly sedate. The relatively austere administration of President Polk included both the laying of the cornerstone of the Smithsonian Institution on May 1, 1847, and the violent Mexican War. One important change occurred in the White House, the installation of gas lights. The Polks also added a porcelain dinner service, of which a plate ornamented with a rather freely interpreted shield from the United States' Seal is shown on page 36.

The Mexican War gave impetus to Zachary Taylor's election to the Presidency, and his short term is represented in the White House Collection by a token of his leadership at the Battle of Buena Vista, the engraved gold cane head shown on page 36. Also representing President Taylor in the White House are the boldly cast brass andirons (page 36), which illustrate the transition from the classical toward the Victorian tastes.

Taylor's term of office was cut short by death, and the Presidency was inherited by Millard Fillmore, whose wife established the first White House library, in the second-floor Oval Room. This room, seen opposite at a later date, was furnished in a comfortable and carpeted style where Mrs. Fillmore, a retired schoolteacher, could enjoy her piano and her books.

The retiring Franklin Pierces made no great mark on the taste, furnishings, or social precedents of the President's House. Mrs. Pierce mourned the death of three sons, the youngest killed in a train wreck two months before the inauguration. The Pierces are remembered, however, for having encouraged the work of the American author Nathaniel Hawthorne, who wrote a campaign biography of the President and one of whose books was gratefully dedicated to him.

Inside the President's House, James Buchanan proceeded in the next administration to undertake a great house cleaning. The Blue Room, unchanged since 1817, was cleared of everything but President Monroe's pier table; worn-out chairs were sold at auction, others banished to the attic, and a rococo-revival suite, made by Vollmer of Philadelphia, took their place. Of this suite, one piece, a circular ottoman, remains in the White House (page 37); the others furnish a Blue Room setting in the Smithsonian's First Ladies Hall.

The sensitive and somber painting of President Lincoln by G. P. A. Healy, perhaps the best-loved portrait in the White House Collection (page 67), is a reminder of the still grander refurnishings of the 1860's. Mrs. Lincoln was determined to have the President's House furnished in the latest style and best quality, and she constantly petitioned Congress for more money.

Some of the many things she ordered are now in the Lincoln Bedroom (page 128). The carved chair in the Treaty Room (page 140), recently recovered from storage, was probably also acquired at this time. Indeed, it is very similar to the chair in which Lincoln is seated in the Healy portrait.

Lincoln's administration was darkened by the Civil War, and the White House became again the home of the President as Commander in Chief, witnessing such events as the reception of General Grant by

President and Mrs. Lincoln (page 39), shortly before Grant's appointment as General in Chief of the United States Armies; Lincoln reviewing Union troops at the White House (page 38); and soldiers quartered in the great East Room (page 38).

Lincoln's tragic death by assassination, symbolized in the dramatically draped catafalque in the East Room (page 39), removed from the White House a man whose personality is still summoned up by the furnishings he used and the rooms in which he worked. Theodore Roosevelt expressed the thoughts of Presidents before and since when he said:

> I think of Lincoln, shambling, homely, with his strong, sad, deeply-furrowed face, all the time. I see him in the different rooms and in the halls.

The remaining years of the 19th century saw the gradual reunion of the Nation under a variety of administrations. Large families and the ever-extending executive functions taxed the aging White House that had once appeared so large. Vice President Andrew Johnson assumed the Presidency in 1865 and established his Cabinet Room in Lincoln's former office—the Treaty Room now restored with some of its original furniture (page 138).

President Grant's large and ebullient family included the two boys pictured on their way to school in the pony cart (page 40), and brought a new round of Victorian display in the elaborate and colorful renovation of 1873. Those decorations, long since stripped away, are represented by the clock now in the Treaty Room (page 141). The Grants are also remembered by two pieces given to the White House in 1961-1962: a writing table once used by Mrs. Grant and a sofa owned by the Grant family.

It is pleasing to have one of Mrs. Grant's possessions in the White House, for she was one of the few Presidents' wives who were happy there. Tragically enough, the lives of a succession of 19th-century wives of Presidents were torn by illness and death, but Mrs. Grant was to write:

> My life at the White House was like a bright and beautiful dream and we were immeasurably happy. . . . Life at the White House was a garden spot of orchids, and I wish it might have continued forever, except that it would have deterred others from enjoying the same privilege.

The continuing expansion of the United States' role in world politics led to embassies from the most remote lands, including that of the Chinese minister shown below

FIRST CHINESE *ministry to the United States, in 1878, is received by President Rutherford B. Hayes in the Blue Room. The room was first decorated in blue when President Van Buren reupholstered the Monroe furniture in blue satin in 1837. This drawing by H. A. Ogden appeared in* Leslie's Illustrated Weekly *of October 19, 1878.*

ON JUNE 2, 1886, President Grover Cleveland married Miss Frances Folsom, daughter of his former law partner. In this engraving, the Blue Room is adorned with palms; actually the chamber was decorated with masses of roses and pansies.

being received by President Rutherford B. Hayes in the Blue Room.

The strengthening of the country's ties with Great Britain was symbolized in the presentation of a magnificent oak desk. This ornately carved piece was made from the timbers of the British ship *Resolute,* which was icebound and abandoned in the Arctic and found some 16 months later and returned to England by the U. S. Government. Queen Victoria, in a gesture of appreciation, had the desk made and presented to President Hayes.

President Garfield's assassination brought to the Presidency Chester A. Arthur, hardworking and convivial, whose tasteful renovation of the Executive Mansion was the most drastic in the Victorian period. On April 15, 1882, reported the newspapers, "twenty-four wagon loads of furniture and other household articles were sold at public auction." To redecorate the mansion, Arthur called in Louis Tiffany of New York,

the leading craftsman of the "art nouveau" movement, who later described in detail the work he had carried out, including "the opalescent glass screen in the hall, which reached from the floor to the ceiling, [and] had . . . a motif of eagles and flags, interlaced in the Arabian method" (page 95).

At the same time the greenhouse and conservatories were extended and embellished and became a major attraction for visitors and guests (page 23). The flowers not only provided elaborate displays for the President's table, but could turn an entire room of the house itself into a bower—as in the Blue Room, heavily bedecked in the following administration for the marriage of President Grover Cleveland and the lovely Frances Folsom (above).

BENJAMIN HARRISON'S administration, and Cleveland's second administration following it, made eminently clear the need for expansion of the President's

THRONGS OF PEOPLE *who found easy access to the White House are shown in this sketch, "The Office Seekers," by Charles Broughton in* Leslie's Illustrated *in 1893. The noisy crowds were the bane of successive Presidents, until Theodore Roosevelt brought about the renovation of 1902.*

IN CONTRAST *to the noisy interior, the grounds of the White House were peaceful and parklike in the late 19th century. A small forest of trees screened the house from the city.*

House. Of the three plans prepared at Mrs. Harrison's request, the most extravagant was for two new domed wings, for official, social, and executive functions (page 24). Congress never acted on this plan, since the Speaker of the House, for personal reasons, refused to bring it to the floor. It is worth noting, however, that it represents not only the first major effort to give the house new functions, but also the first to bring to it an historic perspective—for one of the two wings was to have been an "historical art wing." It was Mrs. Harrison who began the only continuous historical project connected with the White House: the collection of representative examples of china from previous administrations. An accomplished china painter, she inspired the design that graced the state china of the administration (page 88).

Cleveland's second administration saw a more restrained proposal for expansion of the White House (page 24), though the plan presented still later in McKinley's administration (page 25) returned to the Harrison proposal, presenting slightly less extravagant domes (with cupolas apparently modeled on the Bulfinch cupolas on the Capitol). This concept was again rejected, mainly because the approaching centennial of the Capital City had given rise to a movement, headed by architect Glenn Brown, to restore and expand—on the original plans— not only the White House but the whole city. The next administration saw the flowering of this project.

WITH THE ARRIVAL of the Theodore Roosevelts and six energetic young Roosevelts in 1901, a new era of expansion began, in the President's House and in the Nation. It was effectively symbolized by the first large-scale architectural remodeling of the White House—together with the long-overdue expansion. The White House staff had never seen anything quite like the Roosevelts and

EDITH KERMIT CAROW, *wife of Theodore Roosevelt, appears in Theobald Chartran's fine painting, now in the Green Room. The rosewood table of the Lincoln era (below) was a favorite of Mrs. Roosevelt, who had the new furniture in her bedroom and sitting room stained to match it. The table is today in the Lincoln Bedroom.*

IN A SCENE *reminiscent of the early 19th century, when grazing flocks added a rustic note to the President's Park (page 19), sheep cropped the White House lawn during World War I, in the administration of Woodrow Wilson, releasing men for the war effort.*

THIS HAMMOND *typewriter was used by President Wilson in personally preparing the drafts for his messages and speeches. A former president of Princeton University, Wilson was both philosopher and politician, a scholar and a passionate man of action.*

looked on with fascination at pony rides, roller-skating contests, and a Chinese wrestling match in the East Room, heretofore the scene mainly of receptions, weddings, and funerals. Exasperated by the unbearably crowded second floor, which still contained both the private rooms and the public offices, Theodore Roosevelt called in the fashionable firm of McKim, Mead & White. It was only natural that so strong-willed a man as Roosevelt should turn to the most important and successful architectural firm in the United States. They had created the first major structure of the Colonial revival style, the Taylor House at Newport, in 1886. The senior partner, Charles Follen McKim, was an architectural member of the McMillan Commission, which in the same year brought to a conclusion its study of an exciting new plan for the city of Washington. This plan, like the recommendations for the White House, combined a return to original form (L'Enfant's plan) with an expansion and embellishment of function.

Removing the tangled growth of conservatories and greenhouses on the west lawn, the firm was delighted to find intact most of Jefferson's pavilion of 1807. The long win-

GRACE GOODHUE COOLIDGE had all the attributes of a popular wife of a President; handsome and hospitable, she is seen here in a portrait by Howard Chandler Christy. CHINA ROOM

WELL-TRAVELED *and cultivated, Lou Henry Hoover brought a feeling for history to her role at the White House. This portrait by Brown is copied from the original by Philip de László of 1932.*

dowed galleries they then built to the east and west of the main house followed and incorporated what remained of the old pavilions and culminated in a small white office building on the west which, though planned as a temporary structure, had Palladian windows and other elements in harmony with the original building (page 25).

Inside the mansion, President Arthur's Tiffany glass was stripped away, and the Entrance Hall took on its present-day appearance (page 91). The old stairway in the Main Hallway was removed, and the State Dining Room, enlarged and richly paneled in classically carved oak (page 115), also assumed the form it retains today. For this room the firm designed furniture, most of which is still in the room (page 114), including one large and two smaller side tables with eagle supports which Stanford White modeled on a table in his own home. The fine English stone mantelpiece, removed in the renovation of 1948-52, was duplicated and installed in the summer of 1962.

The East Room, which still bore the signs of its florid 1873 redecoration (page 98), was stripped of its stuffs; carpets and wall coverings vanished to be replaced by the white

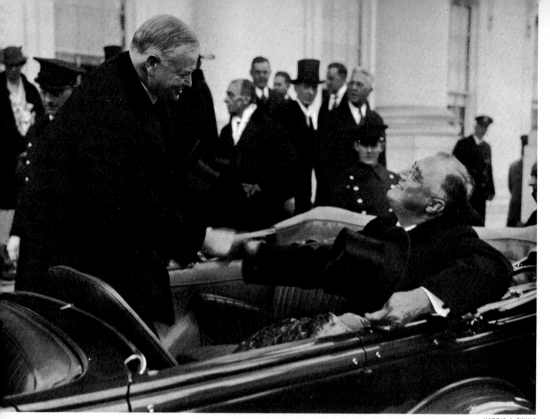

EMPHASIZING *the peaceful passing of power from one administration to the next, President Herbert Hoover greets President-elect Franklin Roosevelt in 1933.*

PRESIDENT HARRY TRUMAN *meets with Great Britain's Winston Churchill in the West Office Wing of the White House. This meeting in January, 1952, occurred shortly before the Trumans returned to the remodeled mansion.*

walls with classical details and the gleaming parquet floors very much as they appear today (page 96). The Blue Room was furnished in a restrained French Classical style reminiscent of the Monroe period, including the large set of chairs which the firm apparently modeled on the general lines of the Bellangé set purchased in 1817.

The same classical approach created the present restrained aspects of the Red and Green Rooms, and two mantels ordered by Hoban during the rebuilding of 1817 were installed in these parlors. The furnishing of these rooms was eclectic, for Mrs. Roosevelt proved faithful to some of the Victorian vestiges, including the marble-topped table (page 45), today in the Lincoln Bedroom, which she loved and kept in her own apartment.

After this overhauling, no great changes took place during the next three administrations. Mrs. Taft was thrilled with her role as the wife of a President, and it is to her love of cherry trees that Washington owes its annual Cherry Blossom Festival. Her enthusiasm for cherry trees, expressed during a visit to Japan, inspired the city of Tokyo to send thousands of trees to Washington to be planted in the reclaimed Potomac Park built around the Tidal Basin.

The scholarly and sensitive Woodrow Wilson, in every respect a lover of peace, nevertheless led the Nation during World War I. He took up his heavy task with good grace. Wilson's ideas and statements were very much his own; he often typed the drafts himself on the Hammond typewriter shown on page 46.

Wilson was succeeded by Warren G. Harding, whose death brought to office Cal-

B. ANTHONY STEWART AND DONALD McBAIN © NATIONAL GEOGRAPHIC SOCIETY

PRESIDENT AND MRS. DWIGHT EISENHOWER *stand in the main stairway with Queen Elizabeth and Prince Philip of Great Britain. The photograph was made before a state dinner given in honor of the royal couple during their visit in 1957.*

vin Coolidge. Although the Coolidges bear the image of restrained New Englanders, with them the house entered the final phase of its development as home and symbol, museum and office—the whole canvas of its meanings today.

Mrs. Coolidge, whose handsome portrait in red evening dress is one of the most admired at the White House (page 47), found the mansion "a home rich in tradition, mellow with years, hallowed with memories." She brought out of storage the bed in the Lincoln room and crocheted for it a bedspread, now in the White House Collection. She was also instrumental in getting Congress to pass a resolution that would allow the acceptance of appropriate antiques for the furnishing of the house.

It was during this period too that, when it became necessary to make repairs to the roof, it was decided to raise it enough to turn the old attic into a full third floor. The remodeling included the glassed-in "sky parlor" over the South Portico.

The knowledgeable Herbert Hoovers, in a period which saw many additional duties and powers develop in the Presidential office, strengthened the mansion's growing symbolism as well.

The Hoovers gathered furniture that dated from the Lincoln and Grant administrations and placed it as a group in a bedroom on the second floor. Four chairs which appear in the contemporary Carpenter lithograph of the first reading of the Emancipation Proclamation were reclaimed from White House storage by President Hoover and used in his office. Today they are in the Lincoln Bedroom (page 130), together with the Earl portrait of Andrew Jackson, admired by Lincoln and also shown in the Carpenter print.

The unprecedented expansion of Government in succeeding decades brought the most significant changes to the house in the rebuilding of the West Wing office building in 1934 and the rebuilding of the East Wing during World War II. Though Franklin D. Roosevelt's administrations were necessarily concerned with the vast problems of depression and war, various historic gifts continued to make their way into the mansion: The sword intended by the French Government for George Washington, but which had not been completed at the time of his death, was presented as a gesture of good will in 1933.

In 1938 Steinway & Sons presented the

"PEACE HAS HER VICTORIES AS WELL AS WAR. . . . *All of us can take pride and satisfaction in this victory of technology and the human spirit." This was President John Kennedy's tribute to astronaut Lt. Col. John Glenn, Jr., on February 26, 1962, after his return from three orbits in* Friendship 7. *Earlier, the President had told a joint session of Congress: "Now it is time . . . for this Nation to take a clearly leading role in space achievement which in many ways may hold the key to our future on earth."*

PRESIDENT JOHN FITZGERALD KENNEDY *lies in state in the crape-hung East Room after his assassination on November 22, 1963. The Honor Guard keeping silent watch included at left a member of the Special Forces developed and expanded by the President. Those paying their respects at the White House included members of Congress, the Judiciary, and the Diplomatic Corps. From the East Room, the casket was removed to the Rotunda of the Capitol where thousands of Americans passed by the flag-draped bier.*

grand piano now in the East Room. Much admired by President Roosevelt, it is appropriately supported by carved eagles.

In 1948 President Harry Truman became concerned about the vibration of floors of the White House, and asked a committee to investigate its structural condition. It was soon found that the new third story and roof of 1927 had been laid on the old and overburdened interior walls, which had progressively settled and cracked. At the same time, channeling away at the original timbers during the continuing changes and improvements of the 20th century had further weakened the framework. Three alternative plans were proposed to meet the situation: two called for the complete demolition of the historic building.

The strength of the house as a symbol to the American people turned the decision to the third proposal. It was the most expensive but also the most saving, for it called for the retention of the original walls and the reinstallation of the interiors against a new steel framework. The White House became a shell (page 27) in which a new and enlarged basement was dug. The house was then put back together with only one major change to the finished appearance of the interior, the new position of the main stairway, which was turned from the Cross Hall into the Entrance Hall on the first floor, to provide a more appropriate entrance for the President and First Lady on state occasions.

PRESIDENT TRUMAN wanted the rebuilt house furnished with antiques and historic items. The budget proved inadequate, and the Trumans moved back into a mansion largely furnished with good copies of antique furniture and with many of the McKim, Mead & White furnishings of 1902.

Among the antiques accepted by the Truman committee was the pair of New England card tables in the Federal style, still in the Green Room (page 100). President Truman was also responsible for initiating the return of several furnishings known to have been in the White House during the Lincoln administration. Among them are a carved rosewood sofa and three matching chairs sent from England in 1954 and placed by Mrs. Eisenhower in the Lincoln Bedroom.

In 1956 the Biddle Vermeil Collection was presented to the White House (page 89), and in 1960 the Diplomatic Reception Room was refurnished in the classic style of the late 18th and early 19th centuries.

Early in 1961, Mrs. John F. Kennedy embarked on a program to refurnish the White House with appropriate antique and historic items. Previous efforts to preserve the Executive Mansion's furnishings for future generations can be traced back to 1889, when Mrs. Benjamin Harrison began assembling china formerly used in the White House.

In 1904, Mrs. Theodore Roosevelt, assisted by Washington journalist Abby Gunn Baker, arranged the growing collection in specially constructed cabinets placed in the Ground Floor Corridor. At that time, descendants of former First Families were encouraged to contribute china and other memorabilia associated with the White House. Because of the success of this effort, it soon became necessary to designate a special area, called the "Presidential Collection Room," to house the acquisitions. Known as the China Room today, its shelves continue to display much of the china received during the early years of this century.

Mrs. Kennedy's first measure was to form in February, 1961, the Fine Arts Committee for the White House. Assisted by leading museum experts and a curatorial staff, the committee developed a philosophy of decoration and furnishing for the mansion. It was realized that the White House could never reflect one period, as do many of our historic homes. Rather it was suggested that a sense of continuity and the process of evolution and growth be emphasized.

By fall, the Fine Arts Committee had made considerable progress in acquiring furnishings for the White House. As a result, the need for paintings of equal significance and quality became apparent. A committee was formed to assemble a permanent collection of paintings, drawings, prints, and sculptures for the Executive Mansion.

In September, legislation was passed by the 87th Congress which provided that "Articles of furniture . . . when declared by the President to be of historic or artistic interest, together with similar articles . . . acquired in the future, shall thereafter be

CONGRESSIONAL LEADERS *and members of the press surround President Lyndon B. Johnson as he affixes his signature to the Civil Rights Act of 1964. At the signing of the bill into law on July 2, 1964, the President proclaimed, "Its purpose is to promote a more abiding commitment to freedom."*

considered to be inalienable and the property of the White House." The act stressed that "primary attention shall be given to the preservation and interpretation of the museum character of the principal corridor on the ground floor and the principal public rooms on the first floor of the White House." The law also provided for the loan to the Smithsonian Institution of any object not in use or on display in the White House. Thus, the proper care and study of the collection would always be maintained.

On March 7, 1964, President Lyndon B. Johnson, recognizing the significant efforts initiated by President and Mrs. Kennedy and noting the importance of the continued care and preservation of the historic furnishings, issued an Executive Order establishing the Committee for the Preservation of the White House. In the order, which also provided for a permanent curator, President Johnson emphasized that "...the Committee shall make recommendations as to the articles of furniture ... which shall be used or displayed in the public rooms of the White House and as to the decor and arrangements best suited to enhance the historic and artistic values of the White House."

The results of these renewed efforts, to which donors throughout the country have given so generously, are seen in their historic surroundings in this guide.

Great Art in the White House

THE WHITE HOUSE painting collection began in 1800, the year of the mansion's first occupancy, with the purchase of the full-length portrait of George Washington by Gilbert Stuart (page 28). Over the years it has grown to include portraits of every past President, some of the Presidents' wives, and a smaller group of varied paintings on historical subjects, including "The Peacemakers" by G. P. A. Healy. Since the White House is a symbol of American life and history, as well as the home of Chief Executives, it is appropriate that it contain representative examples of American paintings of all genre, from the 18th century onward.

Because of efforts made in this area during the past few years, it is hoped that a great collection of such paintings will be formed to become a permanent part of the President's House.

A selection of pictures from the growing White House Collection is presented on the following pages.

ONE OF THE FIRST GIFTS *to the Fine Arts Committee for the White House in 1961, the pencil-and-sepia drawing "The Apotheosis of Franklin," is by the French artist Jean-Honoré Fragonard. Made in 1778, it commemorates Franklin's visit to the Louvre.* YELLOW OVAL ROOM

THE FIRST GREAT PAINTING *acquired by Mrs. Kennedy's Special Committee on Paintings is the superb portrait of Benjamin Franklin by the Scottish artist David Martin. Painted from life in London in 1767, it shows Franklin reading near a watchful bust of Isaac Newton.* GREEN ROOM

55

PRESENTED TO THE WHITE HOUSE COLLECTION, 1962

REMBRANDT PEALE PAINTED THIS PORTRAIT OF THOMAS JEFFERSON *in Philadelphia in 1800, the year before Jefferson became President. With the possible exception of a later portrait by Gilbert Stuart, this painting became the most popular image of Jefferson in the United States and Europe. In 1801, under the supervision of the artist, Cornelius Tiebout of Philadelphia made an engraving of the picture that was widely circulated and copied during the 19th century. Jefferson so admired the portrait that he asked Peale to make him a copy.* BLUE ROOM

THIS PORTRAIT OF ALEXANDER HAMILTON *by John Trumbull was a 1962 gift to the White House Collection. Born in the Leeward Islands in 1755, Hamilton studied at New York's King's College (from which Columbia University has grown), served as aide-de-camp to General Washington during the Revolution and later as first Secretary of the Treasury. He was killed in a duel with Aaron Burr. John Trumbull, American artist of the early 19th century, also served in the Revolution and studied in England with the American artist Benjamin West. This painting is a replica by Trumbull, one of nine known, based on the full-length portrait he did in 1804 for New York's City Hall.* RED ROOM

JOHN MARSHALL, *Secretary of State for John Adams, although better known as fourth Chief Justice of the United States, is represented in this portrait by John Wesley Jarvis. An officer in the Continental Army, Marshall later served in the Virginia Assembly and the U. S. House of Representatives. Beginning in 1801, the eminent American jurist served as Chief Justice for more than 34 years, a record without equal. This portrait of Marshall, commissioned by Nathan Morse, a friend and prominent New Orleans attorney, was painted in Philadelphia by Jarvis and was completed in the fall of 1825.* RED ROOM

THIS PORTRAIT OF JAMES MONROE *is one of the most important recent contributions to the White House. Previously attributed to both Rembrandt Peale and Thomas Sully, the portrait is now considered to be the work of Samuel F. B. Morse and may have been painted in the White House. Morse's journal records that he stayed at the White House in December of 1819 and completed a portrait of President Monroe, the temporary studio being in a room next to the President's office. The portrait descended in the Monroe family until the first part of this century.* BLUE ROOM

ANDREW JACKSON WAS A GREAT NATIONAL FIGURE *and military hero when John Wesley Jarvis painted this portrait in 1819, ten years before Jackson became President. There are two other portraits of Jackson in the White House Collection, but they both portray him at a more advanced age, near the end of his second term of office. This portrait is presumed to be the first of eight painted of President Jackson by Jarvis, and perhaps is a life study from which the others were copied. Direct descendants of the artist donated this portrait to the White House Collection.* BLUE ROOM

"BIRD'S EYE VIEW OF MANDAN VILLAGE," *in North Dakota, is one of the many paintings in the White House by George Catlin, great American painter of Indians of the trans-Mississippi area.*

CHARLES BIRD KING *was the official painter of Indian visitors to Washington. In 1821 a delegation of Indians was received by President Monroe. Wicked Chief of the Grand Pawnee tribe and Eagle of Delight of the Oto tribe are shown.* **LIBRARY**

"**STILL LIFE WITH FRUIT,**" *signed by Rubens Peale in 1862. Son of the American painter Charles Willson Peale, Rubens was born in Philadelphia in 1784. Known for his still-life and animal paintings, he also managed museums founded by the Peale family in Philadelphia, Baltimore, and New York.* GREEN ROOM

"**NATURE'S BOUNTY,**" *signed S. Roesen, 1850. Severin Roesen, a German, immigrated to New York and lived for a time in Williamsport, Pennsylvania.* GREEN ROOM

JOHN JAMES AUDUBON, *America's foremost painter of wildlife, intensely disliked sitting for his portrait. "The eyes," he commented, "to me are more those of an enraged eagle than mine." This romantic portrait, showing Audubon clad in a wolfskin coat, was painted in Edinburgh in 1826 by the noted Scottish artist John Syme. Audubon was then in the British Isles seeking a publisher for his paintings of birds, which were to make him world famous. The portrait was later drawn upon for the frontispiece engraving of Audubon which appeared in many of his nature folios.* GREEN ROOM

PRESENTED TO THE WHITE HOUSE COLLECTION, 1962

"VIEW ON THE MOUTH OF THE DELAWARE RIVER" *was painted in 1828 by Thomas Birch, English-born painter and engraver who settled in Philadelphia. After an early career in portraiture, he turned to painting ships and the sea.* YELLOW OVAL ROOM

"NIAGARA FALLS" *was painted by John Frederick Kensett (1816-1872), a founder of the Hudson River school, who helped popularize landscape painting in America. He painted landscapes of New York State and the Middle West.* YELLOW OVAL ROOM

PRESENTED TO THE WHITE HOUSE COLLECTION, 1962

ANGELICA SINGLETON *in 1838 married Abraham Van Buren, son of President Martin Van Buren, and became hostess for the widowed President. A native of South Carolina and daughter of a wealthy planter, she was a distant relative of Dolley Madison, who played the role of matchmaker. The bust beside Mrs. Van Buren shows her father-in-law, as sculpted by Hiram Powers (page 35). It is presently on display in the East Foyer of the ground floor. This portrait, painted in 1842 by New York artist Henry Inman, is one of the finest in the White House Collection.* GREEN ROOM

GEORGE P. A. HEALY'S *distinguished portrait of John Tyler is one of the best paintings of Presidents in the White House Collection.* FAMILY DINING ROOM

THIS PORTRAIT OF PRESIDENT ABRAHAM LINCOLN *was painted by Healy in Rome in 1869 for a Government competition, won by a painting by William Cogswell (also in the White House Collection). The Healy portrait was later acquired by Mrs. Robert Todd Lincoln, who willed it to the Executive Mansion.* STATE DINING ROOM

JOHN SINGER SARGENT'S VIGOROUS PAINTING *of President Theodore Roosevelt is one of the best of the 20th-century portraits in the White House. Painted at the beginning of Roosevelt's administration, the 1903 portrait captures the decisive air of the 26th President.* RED ROOM

PRESENTED TO THE WHITE HOUSE COLLECTION, 1962

WOODROW WILSON *sat for this portrait by the noted British artist Sir William Orpen early in 1919. The President was in France negotiating the Treaty of Versailles with the major world powers, and was happy to join the score of Allied leaders who agreed to sit for Orpen. After his return to the United States, Wilson embarked on a coast-to-coast speaking tour to rally support behind the League of Nations. Unfortunately, the journey's strain proved costly. He returned to the White House in the fall of 1919, never to recover completely from the physical breakdown suffered during his "crusade to the people." Moreover, the following year found the opponents to America's entry in the League victorious.* RED ROOM

AN AGING DOLLEY MADISON *appears in this water color painted about 1840 by an unknown artist. She wears one of her favorite headdresses, a white silk turban. This miniature is similar to other water colors which "the irrepressible Dolley" presented to her many friends and relatives. She was notably popular and greatly admired for her hospitality, first as hostess to President Jefferson, then as First Lady in her husband's administration.*

PRESENTED TO THE WHITE HOUSE COLLECTION, 1962

LINCOLN *and his son Tad are the subjects of this miniature oil by Francis Bicknell Carpenter, (1830-1900). Through the window appears the North Portico of the Executive Mansion. For about six months in 1864, Carpenter resided with the Presidential family, making studies for his now famous painting, "The Emancipation Proclamation," which hangs in the Capitol. It was during that period this miniature was painted.*

PRESENTED TO THE WHITE HOUSE COLLECTION, 1963

JEAN-ANTOINE HOUDON *(1741-1828)*, *foremost French sculptor of his time, carved this life-size marble bust of Joel Barlow in 1804. Early recognized for his outstanding work in portrait sculpture, Houdon executed busts of the most important personages of his day, including Washington, Jefferson, Lafayette, Napoleon, and Franklin. Barlow, shown here in his fiftieth year, is one of only six Americans portrayed by Houdon. He had gained a wide reputation for his leading role in the post-Revolutionary literary and political circles of this country, while his significant contributions abroad earned him honorary French citizenship.* CROSS HALL

PRESENTED TO THE WHITE HOUSE COLLECTION, 1963

CHARLES HECTOR, *Count d'Estaing, (1729-1794), served as admiral in command of a French naval fleet sent to aid the American Revolution in 1778. He prevented many British landings along the northeast coast of the United States, destroying a number of their ships. D'Estaing was in charge of the guard at Versailles at the time of the storming of the palace in 1789. A friend of the Royal Family, he testified at the trial of Marie Antoinette on her behalf, and was guillotined shortly thereafter. This life-size white marble bust, carved in the heroic French style, is of the school of Jean-Antoine Houdon.* GROUND FLOOR CORRIDOR

PRESENTED TO THE WHITE HOUSE COLLECTION, 1962

PRESENTED TO THE WHITE HOUSE COLLECTION, 1962

"INDIAN GUIDES" *was painted by Alvan Fisher, one of the first generation of romantic painters in America. Born in Needham, Massachusetts, Fisher became a pioneer of landscape and genre painting in America.* GREEN ROOM

"CANNONADING ON THE POTOMAC" *was painted by A. Wordsworth Thompson, a war correspondent for* Harper's Weekly, *from sketches made in October of 1861 at a spot on the Potomac near Balls Bluff, Virginia.* RED ROOM

PRESENTED TO THE WHITE HOUSE COLLECTION, 1962

RECENTLY DISCOVERED, *"Philadelphia in 1858" was painted by the Danish immigrant Ferdinand Reichardt. It depicts the corner of Chestnut and Sixth Streets, with the imposing Independence Hall in the background.* GREEN ROOM

"LAST OF THE MOHICANS" *by Asher B. Durand is dated 1857. A founder of the Hudson River school, Durand has been called the "Father of American Landscape Painting."*

PRESENTED TO THE WHITE HOUSE COLLECTION, 1963

LANDSCAPE AND MARINE PAINTER *Fitz Hugh Lane depicts the calm and serenity of "Boston Harbor—1854." Born in Gloucester, Massachusetts, in 1804, and trained as a lithographer, the artist spent most of his life recording America's northeastern coastline from Maine to New York.* YELLOW OVAL ROOM

WINSLOW HOMER'S *water color, "Surf at Prout's Neck" (circa 1893), dramatizes the power of the giant waves beating the granite coast of Maine. Homer spent the last 26 years of his life in this lonely retreat, painting the sea and man's attempts to control its forces.*

PRESENTED TO THE WHITE HOUSE COLLECTION, 1964

PRESENTED TO THE WHITE HOUSE COLLECTION, 1963

CLAUDE MONET'S *"Morning on the Seine" is one of a series of 18 similar views painted by the artist in 1897. Given in memory of President John Fitzgerald Kennedy by his family, the painting hangs in the Green Room.*

JOHN SINGER SARGENT, *an American, was born and spent most of his life in Europe. "The Mosquito Net," painted in 1908, reflects Sargent's ability to solve the subtle problems of movement, light, and form.*
YELLOW OVAL ROOM

PRESENTED TO THE WHITE HOUSE COLLECTION, 1964

JAMES MCNEILL WHISTLER *was one of the first Western artists to feel the influence of Oriental art. This painting, "Nocturne," typifies his concern for the beauty of twilight and darkness.* GREEN ROOM

"**REVERE BEACH,**" *a small water color, was painted in 1896 by Maurice Prendergast. Recently returned from Paris, the artist spent several months at the shore resorts north of Boston depicting seaside pleasures.* QUEENS' BEDROOM

"HOUSE ON THE MARNE" *and "The Forest" are two of eight canvases by the French painter Paul Cézanne left by the will of Charles A. Loeser to the White House Collection in 1952.* YELLOW OVAL ROOM

"FLAG DAY," *which was painted in February, 1917, is one of the many works on the same subject by Childe Hassam.*

In 1883, Hassam went to Paris to study. While there he was greatly influenced by the work of the French impressionists, especially the canvases of Claude Monet. The effect of the impressionists upon Hassam is reflected in later paintings in which he used brilliant colors freely. After he returned from France, he worked as a painter and illustrator. This spontaneous rendering of flag-bordered Fifth Avenue in New York City after a sudden shower reflects Hassam's interest in the effects of light and atmosphere.

PRESENTED TO THE WHITE HOUSE COLLECTION, 1963

Furniture in the White House Collection

THE FURNITURE in the White House Collection falls into two categories: historic pieces, originally purchased for the mansion and still there, and antique and appropriate pieces being acquired today to refurnish the house.

Only a handful of items from the early 19th century survive; the earliest are from the refurnishing of 1817. The majority date from and after the middle of the 19th century. To make up for the absence of pieces from the earlier period, most of the furniture now being acquired dates from the early 19th century. A few later objects have been chosen to meet specific needs.

The illustrations are not intended to be a comprehensive survey of White House furnishings; the objects shown were chosen as outstanding examples of cabinetmaking as well as for their historic associations.

PIER TABLE *by Parisian cabinetmaker Pierre-Antoine Bellangé is the only piece of the set ordered by Monroe in 1817 that has always been in the White House Collection. The table and four chairs, dispersed in the 19th century, are now in the Blue Room.*

THIS MAHOGANY SECRETARY, *located in the private quarters, is attributed to the Baltimore cabinetmaker Joseph Burgess. It is an outstanding example of Baltimore classical-style furniture at the end of the 18th century. Satinwood inlay is used in the delicate tracery of the glass doors and in the consoles of the pediment. The four drawers and two doors of the side compartments are faced with zebrawood, while each glass door has a center oval of mirrored glass.*

ORIGINALLY OWNED *by William Jones, who was Governor of Rhode Island from 1811 to 1817, this New England dressing table is one of the most important additions to the White House Collection. The scrolled mirror supports as well as the unusual inlays are remarkably similar to the work of John and Thomas Seymour, well-known Boston cabinetmakers at the beginning of the 19th century. This dressing table, or bureau, has been placed in the private quarters.*

FOUR SOFAS *in the classical manner illustrate the variety within a single style. The delicate settee, one of a pair now in the Green Room, is probably of New England origin and is covered in cotton material woven about 1820.*

THE SWEEPING CURVE *of the back, ably controlled by the reverse curves of the arm supports, distinguishes this New York sofa in the Diplomatic Reception Room. The back legs rake; the fluted front legs rest on pointed spade feet.*

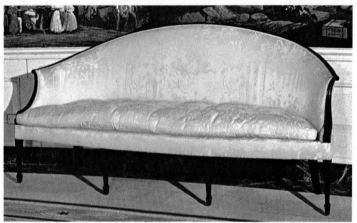

A GRACEFUL CANED SETTEE *with reeded apron, legs, and arm supports is from the workshop of Duncan Phyfe. It has been placed in the Library with a matching settee, four armchairs, and four side chairs.*

THIS UNUSUAL CHAIR-BACK *settee in the Second Floor Hall is from a group including four matching armchairs (four side chairs are still privately owned). It has American secondary woods and is probably from Philadelphia.*

AT LEFT, *one of a group of shieldback chairs of New York origin, with plume and festoon carving on the splat. At right, a Louis XVI armchair, believed to be part of the set purchased by Washington from Count de Moustier for the Green Parlor of Philadelphia's Executive Mansion.*

ALL PRESENTED TO THE WHITE HOUSE COLLECTION, 1962-63

THE CHAIR *on the left with its lattice back and stipple carving is one of four chairs attributed to Samuel McIntire. The armchair at the right is of Philadelphia origin. The back contains elaborate inlay and carving.*

CARD TABLE *in the Red Room is one of a pair attributed to Charles Honoré Lannuier. The winged sphinx support and abundant brass inlay make them the most elaborate of their type.*

PRESENTED TO THE WHITE HOUSE COLLECTION, 1962

WITH MATCHED VENEERS *and bellflower and cockleshell inlays, this card table in the Green Room is typical of Baltimore cabinetmaking in the early 19th century.*

PRESENTED TO THE WHITE HOUSE COLLECTION, 1961

FRENCH EMPIRE *pier table, probably made by the Jacob cabinet shop in Paris, is from designs by Percier and Fontaine. The table, now in the Cross Hall, was made for Napoleon's brother, Joseph Bonaparte, who lived near Bordentown, New Jersey.*

WELL-CARVED *sofa table with fitted writing drawer and gilt winged supports is attributed to Lannuier. In the early 19th century such tables were placed in front of a sofa. Today the table is at the left of the fireplace in the Red Room.*

PRESENTED TO THE WHITE HOUSE COLLECTION, 1961 (ABOVE) AND 1962 (BELOW)

THE ELEGANT *small pier table in the Ground Floor Hall bears a misspelled label: Honore Lanniuer / cabinetmaker, / (from Paris), / keeps his warehouse and manufactory / and cabinetware of the / newest fashion / at No. 60 Broad Street.*

A SPLENDID AMERICAN EMPIRE SOFA, *boldly curved, with carved dolphin side rails and feet. The dolphins are deep green highlighted with touches of gilt.* RED ROOM

A LIGHTHOUSE CLOCK, *one of several signed by Simon Willard of Roxbury, Mass., has an inset medallion of Lafayette.* LIBRARY

WHITE HOUSE COLLECTION

MAHOGANY CENTER TABLE *with gilt brass mounts and marble top has been in the White House since 1817. It is described on the French bill for the Monroe purchases as:* "une table ronde en bois d'acajou. . . ." SECOND FLOOR HALL

LABEL OF JOHN SHAW, *noted Annapolis cabinetmaker, and the date 1797 are affixed to this mahogany secretary. A delicately scrolled pediment with satinwood inlay distinguishes this unique example of the classical period. The lid is decorated with a shell motif while the interior reveals a small center door with an inlay of oakleaf and acorn design. Born in Scotland, Shaw came to the Colonies as an experienced craftsman. His cabinet shop produced furniture for Maryland's House of Delegates and State House.* GREEN ROOM

PRESENTED TO THE WHITE HOUSE COLLECTION, 1963

WHITE HOUSE COLLECTION

REPLICA OF THE DESK *on which James Monroe signed the Monroe Doctrine was added to the White House Collection by Mrs. Herbert Hoover. It is an excellent example of the furnishings Monroe purchased from French cabinetmakers of the early 19th century. The china was made by Dagoty of Paris for the Madison administration (page 87); the butterfly was painted by artist Albert Bierstadt in 1893, during a visit to the White House.*

WRITING-ARM WINDSOR CHAIR *was used by President James Madison after the British attack on Washington. Given refuge in the Quaker settlement of Brookeville, Maryland, Madison sat far into the night of August 26, 1814, dispatching messages to his Cabinet. The comb-back chair was given by a granddaughter of the family that had sheltered the President.*

PURCHASED *for the White House in the Grant administration, this swivel armchair was used in the Cabinet Room until 1902. The chair was sold during the Theodore Roosevelt renovation. It appears in a photograph on page 140.* TREATY ROOM

JOHN ADAMS *originally owned this Sheffield silver-plate coffee urn, a superb example of the refinement and grace of the classic revival. Described in his inventory of 1826, Adams considered it "one of [his] most prized posses- sions." The initials "JAA" (John and Abigail Adams) appear in the engraved ribbon-hung ellipse above the spigot.* FAMILY DINING ROOM

THE CHINA COLLECTION, *housed in the China Room, represents every past President. Mrs. Benjamin Harrison (right) enjoyed china painting and helped design the Harrison administration service; she pioneered the China Collection of the President's House.*

SUGAR BOWL *from a Chinese export porcelain service presented to Martha Washington.*

MADISON *cup and saucer, made by Dagoty of Paris.*

ROCOCO-REVIVAL PUNCHBOWL, *with superb bisque caryatids, probably from the Jackson service.*

SÈVRES TUREEN, *from a set purchased by John Adams.*

MONROE *dinner plate by Dagoty of Paris, about 1817 (top left). Plate from the Haviland state service made in Limoges, France, used in the Lincoln administration, 1861-1865 (upper right). Left, a plate from Grant's Haviland service with a small U.S. Seal in the border decoration, 1869-1877. Right, a plate from the Harrison administration, 1889-1893, made in Limoges. These four 19th-century examples have a definite similarity in form and in the delicacy of the painted decoration.*

WEDGWOOD *(English) plate from the Theodore Roosevelt administration, 1901-1909, at upper left of lower group. Upper right, a service plate from the Lenox china purchased during the term of Wood-row Wilson, 1913-1921. Below left, a plate from the Lenox service ordered during the Truman admin-istration, 1945-1953. Below right, one of the Castleton dinner service plates ordered during the Eisenhower administra-tion, 1953-1961.*

THE VERMEIL COLLECTION, *a group from the extensive silver-gilt bequest to the White House of Mrs. Margaret Thompson Biddle in 1956. The collection, chiefly English and French, covers a wide span, from the Renaissance to the present.*

The selection above includes: Top shelf, either end, Madeira cups, London, 1884; rear center, tray with pierced gallery, by Walker and Hall, Sheffield, 1825; front center, tureen and tray, festoon decoration, by Philip Rundell, English, ca. 1820. Center shelf, left, footed cup engraved "The Agricultural Society of the Hundred of West Derby, to Ann Cockshead, of Lydiate, for raising a crop of potatoes, 1802," marked by Robert, David, and Samuel Hennell; center, French tureen, ca. 1735; right, footed cup, Irish, probably Joseph Jackson, late 18th century. Bottom shelf, left, coffeepot or hot-water pot by Odiot, French, early 19th century; center, monteith, or wine-glass cooler, unidentified marks, ca. 1740; on either side, footed salt, acanthus decoration, London, Philip Rundell, early 19th century; right, pitcher, by Paul Storr, London, ca. 1820.

BRONZE-DORÉ — *The greatest historic treasure of the White House consists of the Monroe purchases of 1817; several mantelpieces, a few pieces of furniture, silver, porcelain, and a splendid group of* bronze-doré *have survived. The vase at left, one of a pair, is described on the French bill as of "forme étrusque." The fruit basket below is listed as one of "2 . . . corbeilles dorées" and origin-inally had candle branches which could be added.*

THIS ELEGANT *11-light candelabrum, one of a pair, is not identified on the 1817 bills, but is seen with the Monroe table ornaments in late 19th-century photographs and may have been added at that time.*

A Guide to the Rooms

THE WHITE HOUSE is the concrete expression of a vision. In many historic houses the moment of greatness has passed and is fixed in time; one must summon up a reflection of vanished grandeur. But in the rooms of the President's House the past lives on to enrich the present; yesterday's greatness is but the prelude to the great moments of today.

In the rooms of this house one draws inspiration for the present and the future, the most enlightened use of a significant past. The living quality of White House history is its greatest power and strength; its symbolism is vital and real to each person, coming for whatever purpose, to any door.

The visitor arriving at the East Gate, the President's caller at the West Wing, a guest at a reception or dinner, entering the south door, a political leader arriving at the North Portico, the President himself coming through any of the many doors cannot but be struck by the noble and active history that still lives in this house. The rooms illustrated on the following pages occupy four floors of the White House (two additional floors lie below ground level).

It is unlikely that the visitor, be he tourist or state guest, would see the whole house. It is hoped that in these pages the vicarious visitor will comprehend the President's House as a meaningful entity.

The first account of the city of Washington was printed in 1791. It was then a city of plans, one year before the laying of the cornerstone of the President's House, but the citizens of the new Republic had already seen a splendid vision of a Federal City which would combine "everything grand and beautiful . . . [and] . . . meet the admiration of all future ages." Their dream has indeed become reality.

THE ENTRANCE HALL *as seen from the North Portico, with the Blue Room beyond.*

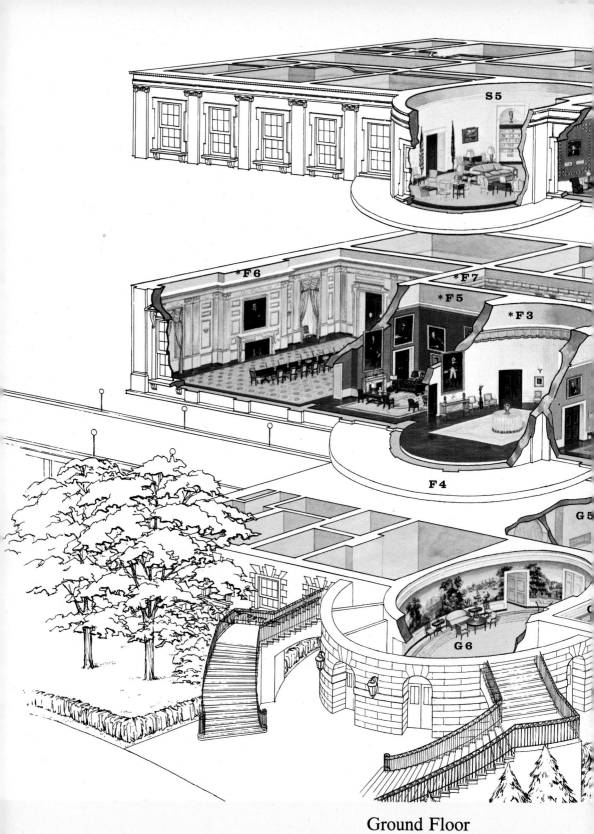

S5

*F6   *F7   *F5   *F3

F4

G5

G6

Ground Floor

A CUTAWAY VIEW *of the*
White House, with the South
Portico in the foreground.
An asterisk marks rooms
open to the public.

*G 1   Library
G 2   Vaulted-arch Corridor
G 3   Vermeil Room
G 4   China Room

G 5   Office of the
      Curator
G 6   Diplomatic Receptio
      Room

First Floor

*F 1	East Room	*F 5	Red Room
*F 2	Green Room	*F 6	State Dining Room
*F 3	Blue Room	*F 7	Cross Hall
F 4	South Portico	*F 8	Entrance Hall

Second Floor

S 1 Queens' Bedroom
S 2 Lincoln Sitting Room
S 3 Lincoln Bedroom
S 4 Treaty Room
S 5 Yellow Oval Room

Robert W. Nicholson

THE ROOMS on the State Floor, which one approaches through the Entrance and Cross Halls, have been modified but not significantly altered since the house was designed and built by James Hoban in 1792. Hoban projected a large Entrance Hall, separated from the Cross Hall by an arcade, and an elliptical salon with flanking rooms beyond. To the right of the entrance was the "Porter's Lodge," today the usher's office.

The lesser stair to the second-floor offices was on the left, and the main double stair was on the west side of the Cross Hall. In 1902 the grand staircase was removed to enlarge the State Dining Room, and a single major stairway to the second floor, today opening into the Entrance Hall, took its place.

The Entrance Hall is furnished in a simple but formal manner with two settees and portraits of Presidents. This spacious entry with marble floor and walls is lighted by a great glass lantern. The Cross Hall leads from the State Dining Room on the west to the East Room; the Red, Blue, and Green Rooms open on the right, or south side, of the hall. The Cross Hall's marble floors and walls were installed in 1948-1952, and decorative plaster panels which date from the renovation of 1902 are inset. Red carpeted,

THE CROSS HALL, *looking from the State Dining Room on the west to the great East Room. The hall is lighted by two 18th-century cut-glass chandeliers.*

PRESIDENT CHESTER A. ARTHUR *had more than 20 wagonloads of furniture sold at public auction in 1882 and called on Louis Tiffany of New York to redecorate the mansion in the emerging style of "art nouveau." The most important installation was the great stained-glass screen in the hall.*

LIBRARY OF CONGRESS

the corridor is brilliantly lighted by two 18th-century cut-glass chandeliers.

The hall is furnished with two large French Empire pier tables (the one at the west end of the hall belonged to Joseph Bonaparte, page 83), and with side chairs and armchairs from the set made in 1902 for the Blue Room, based on the Monroe originals of 1817.

Flanking the door to the Blue Room are two flags, that of the Nation on the left, the President's flag on the right. Between the central pillars in the hall a medallion notes four dates in the building's growth: 1792, the laying of the cornerstone; 1817, the re-

occupation after the fire; 1902, the first large-scale renovation; 1952, the most recent remodeling. In the niches to left and right of the Blue Room are marble busts of Joel Barlow (page 71) and Washington.

Several paintings hang in the Cross Hall. At the west end is Gen. John Stark, New England leader in the Revolution, by Samuel F. B. Morse. Opposite General Stark is a Washington portrait by Charles Peale Polk. At the east end of the hall is a small painting by Chester Harding of Charles Carroll of Maryland, and a portrait of the aged Lafayette by the French court painter Heinsius.

THE EAST ROOM, *decorated in white and gold, serves as a great hall or reception room on state occasions and remains essentially as it was renovated in 1902. Gilt benches are placed against the walls, and a mahogany piano supported by gilt eagles stands on the north side of the room.*

THE EAST ROOM, "the Public Audience Chamber" designed by Hoban, was still incomplete when President and Mrs. Adams arrived as the first occupants of the White House in 1800. So it remained in the first years of Jefferson's administration, when Benjamin Latrobe noted on his plan of the house in 1803 (page 16), "entirely unfinished, the cieling has given way."

In 1807 Latrobe projected a new plan for the State Floor, a plan which may have been carried out, at least in part, in the East Room. The east wall as designed by Hoban had included five windows—the great central Palladian window and two others on either side. Latrobe's plan of 1807 called for the interior closing of the four lesser windows on the east wall (they were to remain as false windows on the exterior façade) and the installation of niches on the new wall expanses, opposite the two original fireplaces in the west wall.

The niches may have been for sculpture, or for the hollow cast-iron figures called "dumb-stoves," fed from furnaces below, which Latrobe is known to have included in other designs. This plan of walling up the four windows was adopted at some point in the 19th century and appears in all known views of the room. The places Latrobe intended for niches were made into fireplaces, and today the interior width of the great central window is still further reduced. Whether Latrobe's vault plan for the ceiling or his other architectural suggestions for the room were carried out in the years before the fire of 1814 is not known.

Little is known of the furnishings of the East Room in James Madison's term, but in James Monroe's administration, the room was furnished with four sofas and 24 chairs, which were refinished and re-covered when President Jackson decorated the entire room in 1829. The bare and unfurnished aspect of the East Room had been noted by many visitors to the President's House before this date. One commented waggishly in the *New York Advertiser* of December 23, 1823, that he had taken an inventory of the East Room and found it contained but "13 old mahogany armed chairs (representing probably the old 13 states), most of which had bottoms, indicating that but few of the

states would ever be found unsafe and useless; and all of them were destitute of any covering, showing that the republican plainness of the revolution should ever be preserved...."

Jackson's remedy for this sorry state of affairs was to order $9,358.27½ worth of furniture from L. Veron and Company of Philadelphia. The bill included: "three 18-light cut-glass chandeliers... one 3-light centre lamp supported by female figures... 4 sets fire brasses, with pokers... 4 bronzed and steel fenders, new style... 4 pier tables with Italian slabs... 498 yds. fine Brussels carpet and border... [and] 24 arm-chairs and 4 sofas, stuffed and covered, mahogany

PRESIDENT MONROE'S CANDELABRA *decorate the two mantelpieces on the south side of the room. They resemble examples by the great French bronze caster Paul-Philippe Thomire.*

work entirely refinished, and cotton covers. . . ."
The bill concluded with 20 spittoons, economically priced at $12.50.

The serene and classic aspect of the room in the early 19th century, with its fluted pilasters and cornices decorated with Greek palmettes, was heavily overlaid with fabrics and Victorian ornaments in the years that followed.

The original ceiling decoration emerges, picked out in gold, from the lavishly refurnished East Room of 1873 (below); the room has been clothed in stuffs and decorative gilt columns added to the interior architecture. The room was again grandly refurnished by President Arthur in 1882, and remained heavily cloaked until the renovation of 1902, when it was returned to classic simplicity.

Though original evidence indicates the salon is more elaborate today than its designers intended, the room with its off-white walls with plaster decoration and parquet floors is in the spirit of the early 19th century.

Basically the same today as it was in 1902, save for new mantelpieces installed in the 1948-1952 renovation, when the chandeliers were also shortened, the room is a lofty, dignified salon, associated with splendid and solemn events. Levees and receptions, weddings and funerals, have taken place there; today it is the first State Room seen by the public visitor on a tour of the White House and the room where guests gather before a great reception or state dinner.

LIBRARY OF CONGRESS

THE EAST ROOM *as decorated by President and Mrs. Grant in 1873. Figured carpet and wall coverings, great gas chandeliers (one of which now hangs in the Treaty Room), and heavy mirrors have been called "steamboat-palace" decor.*

MARK SHAW

AFTER FORMAL DINNERS *at the White House, the East Room is often the scene of entertainments, such as plays, concerts, or recitals. Here in November, 1961, Pablo Casals, the world-famous Spanish cellist, now resident in Puerto Rico, acknowledges the applause of President and Mrs. Kennedy, Governor of Puerto Rico and Mrs. Muñoz Marín, and guests. The full-length portrait of Martha Washington, at left, was painted by Eliphalet Andrews in the late 19th century as a companion to Stuart's Washington at right.*

THE GREEN ROOM, Hoban's "Common Dining Room," became a parlor in the years following Jefferson's administration. Except for early inventories, little documentary evidence exists to indicate how it was furnished in the early 19th century. However, a small piece of cornice decoration, salvaged in the 1948 renovation, a molding in egg-and-dart pattern picked out in gilt, points to the classic mode of interior architecture.

Refurnished by the Fine Arts Committee for the White House, beginning in 1961, the Green Room is now a fashionable parlor as Presidents John Adams or Jefferson might have known it. It represents the graceful and delicate American Federal style, based on English models popular in the late 18th and early 19th centuries.

Architecturally, the room remains as it was remodeled by McKim, Mead & White in 1902. All traces of the successive 19th-century changes in decor were removed, and the room was returned to its original classic style. In the 1948-1952 reconstruction, all the decorative elements of the room were removed but eventually replaced.

The pair of New England card tables on the north wall and the oval worktable to the right of the fireplace were acquired in 1952 after the restoration had been completed.

The crystal chandelier, which until recently hung in the Blue Room, was donated to the White House during the administration of Harry Truman. The remaining furnishings in the room have been acquired since the summer of 1961.

Late in 1962, the walls were re-covered with a moss-green watered-silk material to provide a more appropriate background for the collection of late 18th-century furniture.

One of the recent acquisitions, a secretary desk of Annapolis origin, has been placed between the windows. This excellent example of the classical style is of mahogany with satinwood inlay and bears the label of cabinetmaker John Shaw (page 85).

In each of the long windows on either side of the secretary is a Martha Washington armchair upholstered in cream-and-green silk; the chair on the right is attributed to Joseph Short, cabinetmaker of Newburyport, Massachusetts.

In front of the Annapolis desk stands a French Louis XVI armchair that is believed to have been used by the Washington family in the Executive Mansion in Philadelphia. Washington purchased a set of French drawing-room furniture for the Green Parlor in Philadelphia from Count de Moustier. Matching chairs from this set are found in several American historic house museums. This chair has been placed in the Green Room not only because of its historic significance, but also because White House inventories of the early 19th century substantiate an intermingling of Federal and French style furniture.

In front of the fireplace stands a group of

THE GREEN ROOM — *a Federal parlor in the White House. A classical chandelier with urn shaft and sparkling festoons lights this small drawing room of about 1800. Above the fireplace hangs the famous portrait of Benjamin Franklin by David Martin. The late 18th-century English Axminster carpet is in the classic Adam style.*

GREEN GLASS *and gilt-bronze inkwell, probably of French origin, dates from the early 19th century.*

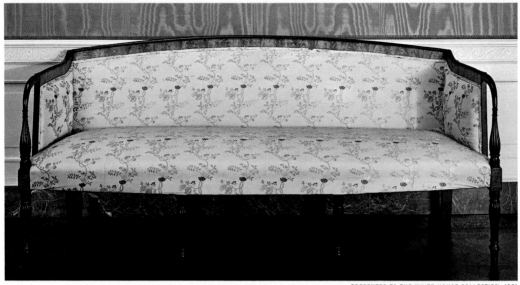

THIS SPLENDID NEW ENGLAND SOFA, *of mahogany elegantly banded with satinwood and covered in a contemporary silk in a classical pattern, was originally the property of Daniel Webster, orator and statesman.*

Federal furniture admirably designed and constructed. The two American settees are covered in early 19th-century embroidered cotton. The graceful urn stands placed between the sofas and the "racquet-back" armchairs are probably of Baltimore origin. The Chinese export porcelain mug on the fireside urn stand is part of a collection of similar porcelain in this room.

Along the west wall of the Green Room stands an impressive New England sofa, once the property of Daniel Webster, flanked by a pair of simple but well-designed Baltimore card tables. On either side of the sofa stands a Martha Washington armchair; these chairs are not a pair but have in common unusually delicate, small-scaled proportions.

An exceptionally beautiful card table stands in front of the sofa. Of the finest Baltimore craftsmanship, it is inlaid with satinwood bellflowers and cockleshells in ovals on the skirt and top.

Two oil paintings hang directly above the sofa: the popular portrait of Mrs. Theodore Roosevelt (page 45) by Theobald Chartran and "Philadelphia in 1858" (page 73), by the Danish immigrant, Ferdinand Reichardt. On either side of the painting by Reichardt is a small still life of fruit; one is by James Peale and the other is signed by Rubens Peale (page 62). The pair of New England card tables on either side of the north entrance are flanked by lattice-back side chairs with delicate drapery and punchwork carving.

With the exception of the portrait of Angelica Van Buren from the White House Collection (page 65), all of the paintings on the north wall have been acquired since the inception of the restoration program for the White House in 1961.

To the left of the door hangs a portrait of the great American naturalist John James Audubon by John Syme, painted in Edinburgh in 1826 (page 63), and "Morning on the Seine," by Claude Monet (page 75).

"Indian Guides" (page 72), a romantic landscape by the American artist Alvan Fisher, has been placed above the door, and below the portrait of Angelica Van Buren is "Nocturne," one of many paintings of this concept by James McNeill Whistler (page 76).

Other paintings in the room which were acquired in 1961 and 1962 are the portrait of Benjamin Franklin by David Martin (page 54); two still lifes by Severin Roesen, hanging above the doors to the East Room; and "A Mountain Glimpse," by Jaspar Cropsey, above the Annapolis secretary.

THE EMPIRE MARBLE MANTELPIECE *in the Green Room is one of a pair ordered by James Monroe after the fire of 1814. In 1902 they were removed from the old State Dining Room and installed in the Green and Red Rooms. Except for a small mantelpiece in a second-floor bedroom, they are the only original ones in the mansion. The* bronze-doré *clock and vases were purchased by Monroe. The fire tools and andirons are American; the latter were made by Richard Wittingham of New York.*

THE BLUE ROOM, AN OVAL DRAWING ROOM, *is the formal reception room in the President's House. The walls are hung in a striped satin material in two tones of cream. A blue-draped valance below the cornice encircles the room. The Blue Room in Benjamin Harrison's administration, 1889-1893 (opposite), shows Monroe's pier table and the Victorian furniture ordered by Buchanan. The room was papered and carpeted in Victorian taste, with cut-velvet upholstery on the chairs and sofas. Through the door to the hall is President Arthur's Tiffany glass screen.*

THE BLUE ROOM, the "elliptic saloon" designed by James Hoban as the central reception room of the President's House, was the building's most elegant architectural feature. The oval end extended into the garden, and French doors, now converted to a window, led for many years to the President's Park, which lay southward to Tiber Creek and the Potomac River. In the fashion of a gentleman's country seat, the south, or garden, front was as important as the north entrance front. Hoban's floor plan projected also an oval portico with circular stair which was not put into effect until 1824.

The elegant form of the oval drawing room was matched by an equally fashionably finished interior. Hoban's plan called for three long windows on the garden, the central one the door, balanced on the opposite end of the room by the door to the hall and two niches, intended probably for sculpture in the classical style. The fireplace on the east wall faced a door, to today's Red Room. It is unknown whether Latrobe's proposed plan of 1807 for the State Floor was carried out, but the Blue Room today resembles his plan more than Hoban's. The sculpture niches were to be eliminated and a columnar screen put across the north side of the room; on the south, two doors were to lead to the Green and Red Rooms, very much as they do at present.

Latrobe also designed, during the Madison administration, a suite of Classic Revival furniture, executed by the Baltimore cabinetmakers John and Hugh Findlay. Drawings exist for low sofas with curved ends and chairs based on Greek forms (page 106). This elegant suite of furniture, so representative of the plans and hopes of the first builders of the President's House, was destroyed in the fire of 1814.

President and Mrs. Madison lived out his second term of office in private residences in Washington while reconstruction of the

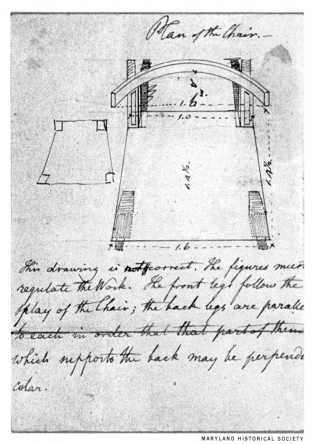

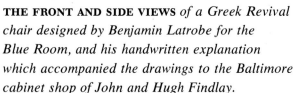

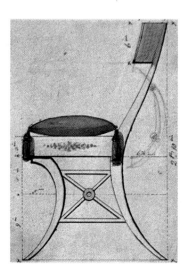

THE FRONT AND SIDE VIEWS *of a Greek Revival chair designed by Benjamin Latrobe for the Blue Room, and his handwritten explanation which accompanied the drawings to the Baltimore cabinet shop of John and Hugh Findlay.*

President's House was in progress under Hoban's direction. In 1817 President Monroe entered the rebuilt but sparsely furnished mansion. An aide, William Lee, had managed to collect a few pieces of furniture from Government inventory, and the remainder had been transferred from the President's temporary quarters.

To make up for this scarcity of furnishings, President Monroe requested Col. Samuel Lane, Commissioner of Public Buildings, to order new furniture for the Blue Room and for the other State Rooms on the first floor. This furniture, ordered through the American firm of Russell and La Farge of New York, New Orleans, and Bordeaux, was made by Parisian cabinetmaker Bellangé.

The suite included a sofa, a pier table, two large looking glasses, two fully upholstered armchairs (bergères), 18 armchairs (fauteuils), 18 side chairs, and two screens, as well as four stools, six footstools, curtains hung over arched gilt poles with eagles in the center, a beautiful rug, and a variety of lighting devices and ornaments in glass, porcelain, and *bronze-doré*. The furniture was covered in pinkish-red silk, ornamented with eagles framed in laurel wreaths.

This main drawing room, with its gilt suite, was the most sumptuously furnished on the State Floor and was intended to impress upon the Nation and the world the renewal of republican strength after the humiliating burning and occupation of the Capital by the British. On January 1, 1818, the President's House was open to the public for the first time since the burning.

For more than 40 years the Bellangé furniture was used in the Blue Room. Although the color of the room was changed numerous times in the 19th century, it was Van Buren who first used blue upholstery in 1837.

In 1860, during the administration of President Buchanan, the still-serviceable French furniture, with the exception of the pier table, was replaced by another gilt set in the rococo-revival style of the Victorian period. The pier table remained in its original position until 1902.

This second set of Blue Room furniture was made by Vollmer and Co. of Philadelphia and was retained until the end of the

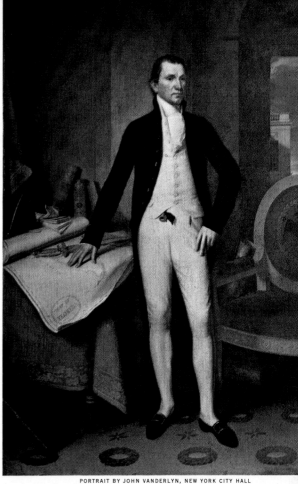

PRESIDENT JAMES MONROE stands beside one of the Bellangé chairs in the Blue Room. Pink-red silk upholstery with classic laurel wreath and eagle and the fine carpet, part of the 1817 furnishings, show clearly. None of the oval-backed chairs are known to have survived.

AN ORIGINAL BELLANGÉ *armchair, returned as a gift, is shown in the Blue Room today.*

THIS PORTRAIT *of President Andrew Jackson by Ralph Earl shows him seated in one of the Bellangé chairs. The original upholstery is again clearly evident.*

McKinley administration. One piece of this furniture, an ottoman (page 37), is on display in the China Room.

In 1902, McKim, Mead & White returned to the more classical tastes of the early 19th century and designed a set of furniture in white and gilt. Chairs from this set are now in the Entrance Hall and the Cross Hall.

The Blue Room was redecorated in the fall of 1962 in a style more appropriate to its collection of Monroe furniture and other objects. The walls have been hung in a striped satin material in two tones of cream, and a blue draped valance trimmed with a tasseled Empire border encircles the room below the cornice line.

The traditional color of blue has been further retained in the curtains and in the upholstery where the woven design is based

on the Monroe originals of 1817. The color also is repeated in the French Savonnerie rug of the early 19th century.

The pier table has been returned to its original position. On it is the white marble bust of Washington based on Ceracchi's model (page 31) just as it appeared in 1817. Above the table is a painting of Washington, one of the portraits of the first seven Presidents which hang in the Blue Room. Two armchairs and two side chairs are from the original Bellangé set.

The superb Empire *appliques* and torchères (page 104) are similar to the bronzes imported from France during the Monroe administration. The French gilt-bronze and crystal chandelier is also early 19th century. The mantelpiece was installed in 1902.

PRESIDENT *and Mrs. Lyndon B. Johnson receive guests in the Blue Room. Designed by Hoban as the principal reception room, and described as the "elliptic saloon" on an early drawing, this oval room with its walls of striped satin is furnished with many of the pieces ordered by Monroe for the White House in 1817.*

THE THREE WINDOWS *of the oval bay of the Blue Room face the President's Park, or South Grounds, of the White House. Beyond the fountain, the Jefferson Memorial appears through the center window, which replaced French doors used as an entrance during a large part of the 19th century.*

THE RED ROOM, "the President's Anti-chamber" in Latrobe's drawing of the State Floor as it looked in 1803, was used as a parlor, or, as the name implies, a waiting room for the President's Library or Cabinet Room next door. Throughout the years it has served as a parlor or sitting room.

In 1877, Inauguration Day fell on a Sunday, and President-elect Rutherford B. Hayes was sworn to the duties of his new office Saturday night in the Red Room, a ceremony that was repeated in the more typical public fashion at the Capitol the following Monday.

Like its sister parlor, the Green Room, the Red Room followed a simple and classic scheme of interior decoration; the cornice, doors, and windows were trimmed with egg-and-dart molding. Although no early engravings exist to document the furnishings of the Red Room in the early 19th century, it is clear from descriptions in contemporary accounts and surviving bills that the room was furnished according to the prevalent fashions—during the Monroe period, in the Empire mode.

The photographs of the latter half of the 19th century show it in heavy Victorian garb, an eclectic mixture of furnishings not entirely relieved by the renovation of 1902, which simplified the remaining rooms on the State Floor. For a period in the late 19th century the Red Room was the favored location for portraits of wives of the Presidents. After the renovation of 1902, the Presidents' wives formed a small gallery of their own, hung by Mrs. Theodore Roosevelt in the Ground Floor Corridor.

Today the room has been furnished as a splendid Empire parlor of 1810-30, stylistically the latest of the three parlors as one walks from the Green Room (1800-1810) through the Blue Room (1817) to the Red Room. Completed in 1962, it was the first of the State Rooms to be entirely refurnished by the Fine Arts Committee.

The walls have been rehung with sumptuous cerise silk with gold borders, specially woven after a French sample of the Empire period, a superb gilt wooden chandelier installed, and a fine red-and-beige Savonnerie carpet placed on the floor. The high quality of the furnishings has been keyed to the splendid original mantelpiece, which had been installed in the State Dining Room in 1817, during the Monroe administration.

Coincidentally, this room contained musical instruments in the early 19th century and is very reminiscent of the Red Music Room at Malmaison, Josephine Bonaparte's house outside Paris, which was furnished in the antique style after the designs of Percier and Fontaine. This long-forgotten era is evoked in the Red Room today by the

THE RED ROOM, *furnished as an Empire parlor of the early 19th century, is hung in cerise silk with gold scroll borders. The fine examples of French and American furniture are placed on a Savonnerie carpet of the Empire period. A great gilt wooden chandelier, with Classic Revival ornament, illuminates the room.*

ANDREW JACKSON, *seventh President, is the subject of this oil-on-ivory miniature, painted during his second term of office. Signed "S. M. Charles, 1835," Jackson considered it to be "one of [his] best portraits." It can be seen in the secretary on the south wall.*

SPHINX-HEAD BRASS MOUNTS *give this fine mahogany Empire sofa an Egyptian motif; it is upholstered in the same silk as the wall covering.*

LABELED BY LANNUIER, *this guéridon is a masterwork of fine inlay, with bronze caryatid heads and a bronze* trompe-l'oeil *marble top.*

inclusion of the little Empire music stand to the right of the fireplace, which holds a spirited air of the early 19th century, "Lafayette's March," written to honor the Marquis on his triumphal tour of 1825.

The Red Room contains excellent examples of both French and American craftsmanship. Between the windows is a great French desk with brilliant ormolu mounts, and in the windows are French Empire torchères—mahogany pedestals set with gilt candle branches. On either side of the desk stands a rosewood chair, in the transitional Empire-Victorian taste, sold at auction after the Lincoln administration, and recently returned to the White House (opposite). Over the desk hangs a splendid convex mirror recovered from White House storage and probably of the Jacksonian era (opposite). On the desk itself is an historic inkstand: a recent gift to the White House, it is the only object there used by our third President, and bears the inscription "T. Jefferson, 1804" (page 30).

To the left of the fireplace is one of the rarer forms in American furniture, a sofa table. This is a splendid work with two soaring winged supports, attributed to the French cabinetmaker who worked in New

York from 1803 to 1819, Charles Honoré Lannuier. The table is flanked by two fine French armchairs, and on it stand a Parian-ware bust of Henry Clay and a small ver-meil monteith from the Biddle Collection in the White House, used as a flower holder. In the fireplace are a pair of gilt-bronze *chenets,* or andirons, stamped by the French bronze caster Gouthière, a pair of Ameri-can fire tools, and an English coal hod, now used as a wood bucket. On the mantelshelf stands the 18th-century French musical clock presented by President Vincent Auriol of France in 1952.

Placed to the right of the fireplace is a graceful Empire sofa with gilded dolphin feet (see mirror, right). Behind this sofa is an unusual American Empire card table with lyre and swan supports and glass mounts.

A pair of impressive American card tables with great winged sphinxes, also attributed to Lannuier, stand on either side of the north door. The tables are flanked by typical graceful American Empire side chairs of the 1820's and also are ornamented with vermeil pieces from the Biddle Collection. Against the east wall stands a remarkably beautiful Empire sofa with bronze sphinx heads un-der the arm supports, perhaps the finest such American piece known today in its sophisticated design and form (opposite).

On either side of the sofa is a well-made American card table of New York origin. The columnar supports and the bases are decorated with stencil designs and gilt. The table on the right holds a particularly fine French bouillotte lamp with original gilt and green tole shade. Drawn up to the sofa are a pair of fine French armchairs, mates to the one at left of the fireplace, and between them is the masterpiece of American Em-pire furniture in the White House Collec-tion, the marble-topped guéridon, labeled by Charles Honoré Lannuier.

This interesting work, the only such form presently identified with an American cabi-netmaker, is based ultimately on Roman bronze examples discovered in the ruins of Pompeii and Herculaneum. The piece is admirably carved and inlaid and is notable for the *trompe-l'oeil* marble top, made prob-ably to exhibit marble pieces gathered by an early 19th-century collector (opposite).

THE RED ROOM REFLECTED *in the great convex mirror, part of the early 19th-century White House furnishings.*

THIS ELEGANT ROSEWOOD CHAIR *has a well-documented history of use in the White House during the Lincoln era.*

STATE DINING ROOM – The very large dinner party, an increasing necessity for the head of state, proved an ever more pressing problem to Presidents and their wives as the 19th century progressed. Hoban's plan had provided a "common" and a "public" dining room; Latrobe's plan of 1807 would have allowed only a single dining room.

Hoban's common dining room, today the Green Room, soon became a parlor, while the two rooms of equal size on either side of the main staircase, on the west side of the house, became the State and Family Dining Rooms (the State Dining Room, the south-west, the Family Dining Room, the north-west, corner).

The Family Dining Room was ample for a succession of Chief Executives, but for large state dinners long tables were set up in the Cross Hall, a drafty and crowded arrangement, or in the East Room, which was referred to in Keim's *Illustrated Handbook* of 1876 as the "Banqueting Room."

The renovation of 1902, by removing the west staircase and including part of the central corridor, enlarged the old State Dining Room to its present spacious proportions and turned the room's axis in the opposite direction. The two matching Italian marble mantels installed during the 1817 rebuilding were removed to the Red and Green Rooms (page 103); the second window of the old room was closed on the inside, and a larger mantelpiece carved of Yorkshire stone was placed in this new wall space.

The enlarged room was completely re-paneled in carved natural oak in the classical style. Fielded panels were set between Corinthian pilasters, a frieze of delicately carved sheaves and festoons ran around the room under the cornice, while cornice and ceiling formed a contrast of white plaster ornament.

The mantel design called for lions' heads carved at either side; these were changed to buffalo heads at the request of Theodore Roosevelt, who preferred a native American animal. This boldly carved mantel, removed in the renovation of 1948-1952, has been duplicated and installed.

The present furnishings of the State Dining Room include the high-backed chairs in the Queen Anne style, ordered by McKim, Mead & White in 1902, and the three consoles, now painted white and gold, supported by eagles in the English Regency manner. The latter were built from sketches by Stanford White based on an antique table in his possession. The large classical style banqueting table was presented to the White House during the renovation of 1948-1952.

In 1961 the room was repainted white and the large chandelier and the wall sconces, all dating from the 1902 renovation, were gilded.

SUPERB BRONZE-DORÉ *plateau and baskets ordered by Monroe are the chief table ornaments in the State Dining Room. The candelabra in the rococo-revival style are from a later administration (page 90).*

THEODORE ROOSEVELT'S *State Dining Room as created and decorated in 1902 by McKim, Mead & White.*

THE STATE DINING ROOM *today with the table in a horseshoe arrangement for a state dinner. The table is set with china ordered during the administration*

of President Harry Truman. The well-known portrait of Abraham Lincoln painted by G. P. A. Healy in 1869 hangs above the white marble mantelpiece.

THE FAMILY DINING ROOM, presently located in the northwest corner of the President's House, was in 1803 the "Public Dining Room," the larger of the two dining rooms provided by James Hoban's design for the State Floor. Latrobe's plan of 1807 proposed a bedchamber with alcove bed in Jeffersonian style, dressing room, and water closet in this space, but it is uncertain if these and the other changes indicated for the first floor of the mansion were put into effect.

At some point in the 19th century this room acquired its present-day role, and the room across the stair hall, the Library or Cabinet of Jefferson's administration, became the public dining room. As neither room was very spacious, the Cross Hall or the East Room was pressed into service for large-scale dinners.

On Hoban's original floor plan, and in the Latrobe drawing of 1803, the room had two windows and a matching fireplace on the western side and formed a bigger, brighter space. During the 19th century a butler's pantry was added on the west. This modification is indicated on Thomas U. Walter's plan for the Executive Mansion of 1853, and indeed may date from that time. The same room arrangement is noted on a floor plan of the 1880's and certainly existed at that date.

A new wall with service door to the pantry and a matching blind door replaced the former window wall. The decorations and furnishings of the Victorian period show the typical use of floral carpets, wall coverings, cloth, and fringe. The photograph of the interesting group (below), made by Frances Benjamin Johnston in 1889, illustrates the furniture and decorative accessories in use at that time.

The mid-19th-century white marble Victorian mantelpiece is curtained in fringed velvet, and on the shelf two of the gilt-bronze candelabra, ordered by President

THE FAMILY DINING ROOM *on the State Floor is furnished with American pieces of the Federal period. A gilt convex mirror crowned with an eagle hangs above the white-and-green-marble mantelpiece. The picture above shows the room in 1889, furnished with pieces in successive Victorian styles and lighted by a many-globed gas chandelier.*

119

PRESENTED TO THE WHITE HOUSE COLLECTION, 1962 (ABOVE AND RIGHT)

MAHOGANY BREAKFRONT,
*one of two made for the
Willing family of Philadelphia
about 1800, is an outstanding
addition to the White House
Collection. The blue-and-gold
china was purchased during
the administration of
President Benjamin Harrison.*

ORIGINAL BRASS PULL
*from the sideboard in the
Family Dining Room
commemorates the death
of the first President of
the United States.*

Monroe in 1817 and today in the East Room, can be identified. On either side of the mantel stands a marble-topped pier table with mirror back, one of which was recently recovered from White House storage. This surviving piece in late Empire style bears the label of Anthony Quervelle, cabinetmaker, who worked in Philadelphia and is listed in the directories of that city between 1835 and 1849. The piece may date from the Van Buren administration.

The many-globed gas chandelier hangs over a round table with gadrooned border and hairy paw feet, here covered with a long white cloth. The chairs around it and in other parts of the room are of an earlier style; they may have been purchased during the Grant administration or in a still earlier period. The sideboard on the south wall is typical of the late 19th century in proportion and detail and holds a number of identifiable objects, including two punchbowls and two fruit baskets from the Lincoln service; pieces of china from the Hayes administration, including the turkey platter on the central shelf, now in the China Room; and the silver boat, which is also still in the White House Collection.

In 1902 the extensive remodeling of the western side of the State Floor, during the McKim, Mead & White renovation, with the removal of the main stair to the other side of the house and the creation of the present State Dining Room, also included today's scheme of decoration in the Family Dining Room. The vaulted ceiling and the cornice with its frieze of classical motifs date from the 1902 renovation. The room continued to serve as the private dining room for the President's family until 1961, when another dining room was created on the second floor.

Today the Family Dining Room serves as a small State Dining Room for breakfasts and luncheons; it has been redecorated and refurnished in the classical style suitable to the date of the mansion itself. The painted yellow walls are accented by the white woodwork and decorative plaster cornice.

The room contains several pieces of American Federal furniture in the styles of Sheraton and Hepplewhite. The oval ends of the mahogany pedestal dining-room table (page 118) have fine reeded saber legs, and a group of Sheraton-style side chairs surrounds the table.

There is a notable sideboard in this room with a tambour central door framed in a simulated drapery arrangement. One of the original brass pulls embossed with the profile of George Washington is seen on the opposite page. A mahogany breakfront (opposite), one of a pair made in Philadelphia in

the early 19th century, has been placed in this room and contains the blue-and-gold china dating from the administration of President Benjamin Harrison (page 88).

On the white-and-green-marble mantelpiece stands a French clock of the early 19th century, decorated with a standing figure of Washington and an American eagle and other symbols of the new Republic. This clock, made by Dubuc in Paris, was presented to the White House Collection in 1961. Hanging above the mantelpiece is a convex gilt mirror, probably made in New York in the early 19th century and donated to the White House in 1962.

A painting by Edward Troye of General Cocke, of Bremo, Virginia, and the G.P.A. Healy portrait of President John Tyler (page 66) hang in this room. The cut-glass chandelier and matching wall sconces are of English origin and date from the last half of the 18th century.

BRIG. GEN. *John Hartwell Cocke of Bremo, Va., mounted on his horse Roebuck. Completed in 1859 by Edward Troye, noted recorder of American sporting history, this painting depicts Cocke at the time of the War of 1812.*

DIPLOMATIC RECEPTION ROOM, an oval room on the ground floor, is used as the entrance to the mansion by the President and his family and guests at state functions. It is furnished as a stately parlor or drawing room of the late 18th or early 19th century. The ground floor has only gradually acquired its present role and status in the 20th century; it was originally the basement and contained the kitchen, laundry, and similar functional workrooms.

The present Diplomatic Reception Room is shown on 19th-century floor plans as a boiler and furnace room. In the renovation of 1902, as part of the attempt to relieve the crowding, a new basement was dug and the ground-floor rooms finished to serve the needs of the family and staff. The reception room soon became a sitting room and continues to serve this purpose.

Franklin Roosevelt used this room for his famous "fireside chats," in which he broadcast messages on the state of affairs at home and abroad to the country at large. Strangely enough, the room has no usable fireplace.

In 1960, during the Eisenhower administration, the room was furnished with excellent examples of American craftsmanship. A rug in the Aubusson manner was woven, incorporating the seals of the 50 States. The sofa, chairs, and tables, of New York and New England origin, are in the appropriate classical or Federal style. The light cream-colored carpet and furniture upholstered in shades of yellow create a color scheme of elegant gold and white, also popular in the early years of the Republic.

In 1961, additional American furnishings of the early 19th century were donated and the room was completed with the presentation of the superb paper, "Scenic America," printed by Zuber & Co. in Rixheim, Alsace, in 1834. This historic paper, based on engravings of the 1820's, contains several views of American natural wonders particularly admired by Europeans: Niagara Falls, the Natural Bridge of Virginia, Boston Harbor, West Point, New York Bay, and Lake George in upstate New York. Photograph (opposite) shows the bustling port of Boston.

Scenic paper was popular in America in the 19th century; indeed, paper was the typical wall covering in the White House at that period. As this type of interior decoration was not yet represented at the White House and as the oval shape of the room seemed particularly suited to the panoramic sweep of the scenic views, this installation has had a happy dual purpose and effect.

DIPLOMATIC RECEPTION ROOM *on the ground floor. This spacious room with its panorama of scenic wallpaper serves as the entrance to the mansion for the President's family and for guests at state functions.*

PRESIDENT FRANKLIN ROOSEVELT *in the Diplomatic Reception Room, from which he broadcast the famous "fireside chats."*

HARRIS AND EWING

THE WHITE HOUSE LIBRARY *was restored and refurnished in 1962
in the classical style of the early 19th century. The red tole and crystal
chandelier was once owned by the family of James Fenimore Cooper.*

THE LIBRARY, on the ground floor of the mansion, recently has been redecorated and refurnished in the classical style. As today's ground floor was originally the basement, the Library did not exist as a room until the 20th century. In the renovation of 1948-1952, the Library was one of a number of rooms on the ground floor refinished with paneling cut from timbers removed from the interior of the building.

The present decorative scheme is that of a painted room of the early 19th century. It was fashionable in the Federal period for rooms to be painted in light shades of cream, buff, gray, and similar tones. As the three parlors on the State Floor, the Red, Blue, and Green Rooms, are traditionally hung in silk, it was impossible to illustrate this typical and representative scheme of early American decoration there.

The Library, with its walls painted a distinctive and delicate pale yellow, and moldings picked out in lighter cream color, now serves as an excellent example of the painted room.

A mantel, appropriate to the same era, has been installed. Removed from a house in Salem, Massachusetts, it is attributed to the cabinetmaker Samuel McIntire. Its applied plaster decoration of classical figures, bowknots, festoons, and pendent bellflowers has also been painted cream and stands out in relief against the pale yellow of the mantel. Over the mantel hangs an oil sketch, "The Signing of the Declaration of Independence," by the 19th-century French painter Edouard Armand-Dumaresq.

The room is furnished with a splendid and well-documented set of caned furniture made by Duncan Phyfe, popular and notable cabinetmaker of the early 19th century who kept a large shop in New York. In the center of the room stands an unusually large octagonal library table supported by a pedestal base of three legs. This table also is of New York origin.

Five oil portraits by Charles Bird King of an Indian delegation that came to the White House in 1821 have been placed in the Library. The chandelier of red tole and crystal was once owned by the family of the American novelist James Fenimore Cooper. The urn-shaped French vase in the window sill (opposite) is one of two given by Lafayette to Governor Eustis of Massachusetts in 1824. A wood floor, typical of the Federal period, has been carefully laid over the existing marble and partially covered with an excellent Aubusson carpet.

In 1962, a committee was formed for the purpose of selecting a library of works representative of American thought and tradition. This recently completed project has added more than 2,700 volumes to the White House collection, almost completely restocking the room's shelves. These books were given through the generosity of private citizens and publishers alike.

GEORGE WASHINGTON, in 1790, ordered a group of recently patented Argand lamps, noting that they were said to "consume their own smoke . . . give more light, and are cheaper than candles." A 1962 gift, this silver English 18th-century model was one of a pair presented by Lafayette to General Knox, of New York. The lamps are located on each side of the fireplace.

WHITE HOUSE COLLECTION

THE YELLOW OVAL ROOM

THE YELLOW OVAL ROOM on the second floor of the White House, directly above the Blue Room, has served many purposes in the history of the Executive Mansion. The room has been used by numerous Presidents as an office, by others as a bedroom, library or a private study, and as a private sitting room. It is for the latter use that White House architect James Hoban originally intended the room.

Early White House inventories and accounts of visitors to the Executive Mansion reveal much of the room's appearance in the early 19th century. In their brief one-year

tenure at the White House, John and Abigail Adams procured some furniture for the room. An inventory taken in the last year of Jefferson's administration indicates it was by then a drawing room containing many objects in the French Louis XVI style.

In 1809, under the guidance of Dolley Madison, the furniture in this room, known then as the Ladies' Drawing Room, was upholstered in yellow damask, and curtains with festoons and fringes were made of the same material.

The color yellow has been repeated in the recent redecoration of this room. The furni-

ture was donated to the White House in 1962 and, in the tradition of Thomas Jefferson, is predominantly in the Louis XVI style. The *bronze-doré* chandelier is hung with chains and drops of rock crystal, as are the candelabra mounted on the columns between the windows.

To the right of the fireplace hang Thomas Birch's "Mouth of the Delaware," and "Boston Harbor," painted in 1854 by Fitz Hugh Lane. On the west wall are two of eight paintings by the French impressionist Paul Cézanne that were bequeathed to the White House. Among the finest paintings in the collection, both have been placed in this room where the President receives his most distinguished visitors. The remaining six hang in the National Gallery of Art.

Before a state dinner at the White House, the heads of state meet in this room. In the right of the picture (opposite), the flag of the United States and the Presidential flag are mounted on standards. When the President and his guests of honor descend the grand staircase to the State Dining Room, the colors are removed and carried ahead of the party to the ruffles and flourishes of the Marine Band in the Entrance Hall.

THE YELLOW OVAL ROOM *is furnished in the French style of Louis XVI so favored by Thomas Jefferson. A portrait of George Washington by Rembrandt Peale, in his porthole style, hangs above the white marble mantelpiece.*

ONE OF A PAIR *of vases purchased by Monroe in 1817. On both vases appear painted scenes of Homer and Belisarius; the vases are attributed to the French manufacturer P. L. Dagoty.*

127

THE LINCOLN BEDROOM, *on the second floor, was originally Lincoln's Cabinet Room; here he signed the Emancipation Proclamation in 1863. The two velvet-covered slipper chairs on each side of the bed were sold after the Lincoln administration and were returned in 1961 to the White House.*

THE LINCOLN BEDROOM, which is associated with the 16th President because it once served as his Cabinet Room, bears the following identifying plaque on the mantelpiece:

IN THIS ROOM ABRAHAM LINCOLN SIGNED THE EMANCIPATION PROC-LAMATION OF JANUARY 1, 1863 WHEREBY FOUR MILLION SLAVES WERE GIVEN THEIR FREEDOM AND SLAVERY FOREVER PROHIBITED IN THESE UNITED STATES.

The east end of the second floor, where the room is located, once contained all the public offices, waiting rooms, and conference chambers, while the private living quarters of the President and his family lay on the west side of the same floor.

The overcrowding and noise resulting from this dual purpose of a single story led successive Presidents of the later 19th century to ask for remodeling of the house. The renovation of 1902 removed offices to the new West Wing. The space thus made available is occupied today by the upper stair hall of the main stair, the Treaty Room, the Queens' Bedroom, the Lincoln Bedroom, and the Lincoln Sitting Room.

The room as it existed in Lincoln's time is known by at least three contemporary pictures. An early photograph of President Lincoln in the room shows part of the fireplace wall and the figured carpet and wallpaper the room then contained. The other two are the well-known painting of Lincoln's Cabinet by Francis Carpenter, after which many engravings and lithographs were made, and the little-known and by far the most detailed and revealing room view shown in the drawing on page 130.

This drawing, made by C. K. Stellwagen in October, 1864, before Lincoln's second election, described this Cabinet Room as "facing the Potomac, and Washington Monument" and noted that "the armchair over by the window (black hair cloth) is that of the President. The other furniture is faded blue Rep. Wallpaper, dark green with a gold star. Doors, imitation mahogany, with white frames. Carpet, dark green with buff figure in diamonds. Portrait over the mantel is Gen. Jackson." Prints of all three of these

contemporary views are in the White House and are an incomparable aid in the room's gradual restoration.

Some of the most important objects that were in the room, such as the Cabinet chairs, the sofa, and the Earl painting of Andrew Jackson, remain in the collection of the President's House. An observer in 1862 noted that the room "is very neatly papered, but should be better furnished. All the furniture is exceedingly old, and is too ricketty to venerate."

The furniture in the Lincoln Bedroom, all of the Victorian period, came chiefly from White House storage. Eight pieces that have Lincoln associations came from outside the White House: They are the clock, the sofa and three matching chairs, the desk, and the two slipper chairs. In general, the surviving White House pieces are of the 19th century, and while not all can be clearly documented as in use during Lincoln's administration, they are close to that era.

THIS CLOCK, *of the late Empire period, stands on the mantelpiece in the Lincoln Bedroom. It is similar to others purchased during the Jackson administration.*

ANDREW JACKSON *portrait, attributed to Ralph Earl, was admired by Lincoln and hung in this room during his administration; this fact was observed in contemporary prints and the picture returned to the room. The two chairs, part of a group of four which has survived in the White House, were also used by Lincoln in his Cabinet Room. The 19th-century table is from the White House Collection.*

THIS LITTLE-KNOWN *sketch by Stellwagen, of Lincoln's Cabinet Room, is the clearest and most revealing contemporary view. A description written below the sketch identifies some of the objects and notes that the wallpaper was dark green with gold stars.*

Some pieces, such as the Cabinet chairs, are clearly of an earlier period, possibly 1830-1840, but were made notable by their use in Lincoln's time. The bed and round table seem to have been purchased in his administration; a bill of May, 1861, describes two similar pieces. However, they were not in the President's own room but in the guest room. The same observer mentioned above wrote in the San Francisco *Daily Alta California* of May 12, 1862:

> The guests' room, now known as the Prince of Wales' room [Queen Victoria's son had visited the United States during the Buchanan administration], since that youth occupied it, has been thoroughly ornamented and refurnished. . . . The principal feature of the room is the bed. . . . The head board is a piece of rich carved work, rising eight feet above the bed, and having an oval top. Twenty feet above the floor . . . is a magnificent canopy . . . from which the drapery hangs in elegant folds, being in the form of a crown, the front ornament upon which is the American shield with the Stars and Stripes carved thereon. . . .

This description seems to fit the bed now in the Lincoln Bedroom (the draped canopy with carved shield is shown in photographs of the late 19th century), and the same writer recorded "the centre table . . . of solid carved rosewood . . . quite costly, and exceedingly beautiful." The President's own apartment, as one would suspect, was furnished in simpler, more modest fashion.

A number of interesting objects have been added to the room: a collection of old books, the titles known to have been used by Lincoln; a painting of a mid-19th-century family; and a portrait of Lincoln by Douglas Volk, on loan from the National Gallery.

THIS HOLOGRAPH COPY *of Lincoln's Gettysburg Address, one of five made by the President from his original, is the only one titled, signed, and dated: November 19, 1863. It was made at the request of the American 19th-century historian George Bancroft, and a facsimile was auctioned to raise money for Civil War soldiers at the "Sanitary Fair" held in Baltimore in 1864.*

THE QUEENS' BEDROOM, also known as the Rose Guest Room, is located on the second floor of the White House. Just as the Lincoln Bedroom serves for male dignitaries, the Queens' Bedroom has been assigned to distinguished ladies, including five queens: Elizabeth of Great Britain (the present Queen Mother), Wilhelmina and Juliana of the Netherlands, Frederika of Greece, and Elizabeth II of Great Britain. The room has for some years been decorated in shades of red, rose, and white; the present curtain and bed hangings continue this tradition. With its adjacent dressing room and bath, it is a comfortable and spacious apartment.

The bed is said to have belonged to Jackson. Although it has not been possible to document its history, the bed resembles Southern samples in the late Sheraton style and dates probably between 1820-1840. It was presented to the White House in Theodore Roosevelt's administration. The shield-back chair near the window is of New York origin and was presented to the White House Collection in 1962.

The mahogany bookcase secretary be-

THE QUEENS' BEDROOM *on the second floor is decorated with rose-patterned material. Elizabeth of Great Britain (the present Queen Mother), Wilhelmina and Juliana of the Netherlands, Frederika of Greece, and Elizabeth II of Great Britain have stayed here.*

EARLY 18TH-CENTURY *English overmantel mirror and three-part looking glass presented by Queen Elizabeth II, during her visit as a princess in 1951.*

tween the windows was given to the White House in 1962 and dates from the end of the 18th century. The English looking glass above the mantel, with its scrolled gilt border and floral painting in the early 18th-century manner, was presented by Elizabeth II of Great Britain, when, as a princess, she visited Washington in 1951 with Prince Philip. Since the White House was undergoing renovation, the royal couple were entertained by the Trumans at Blair House.

On November 3d, the last day of her visit, in the White House Rose Garden, Princess Elizabeth presented the overmantel mirror to President Truman for the White House on behalf of her father, King George VI. She spoke words well worth hearing again:

> The renovation of the White House has attracted interest all over the world. Everyone knows how closely it has been bound up with the history of your country and how important it is to your people as a symbol of national pride. . . . We are glad to join with you in celebrating its restoration. My father . . . has wished to mark the event with a personal gift. . . . The work of 18th-century artists. . . . It is his hope, and mine, that it will be a welcome ornament to one of your proudest national possessions, and that it will remain here, as a mark of our friendship, so long as the White House shall stand.

THE EMPIRE GUEST ROOM is the first of the White House guest rooms to be redecorated and refurnished during the current restoration project; it contains a number of objects of particular historic interest. The President's House as originally built had two stories and an attic; in 1927 the roof was repaired and raised to provide much-needed guest and servants' rooms, as well as the "sky parlor," the sunroom loved by Mrs. Calvin Coolidge. The new floor was concealed as much as possible behind the gallery that frames the roof, so that the outer appearance of the house would remain unaltered.

The small corner room has been newly hung and the furniture upholstered in red and white printed cotton, a contemporary version of the French early 19th-century *toile de Jouy*. This pattern, depicting events in the career of Benjamin Franklin, has among other inscriptions a banner with the inspiring words: WHERE LIBERTY DWELLS THERE IS MY COUNTRY. This printed fabric, originally called *Hommage à Franklin,* is partially based on the drawing by Fragonard now in the White House Collection, page 55. In addition to reminding the visitor of one great American, the room also honors two others. A superb collection of early engravings of George Washington has been hung on the walls, and a bronze statue of the first President stands on an Empire washstand. The bed in this room, on loan from the United States National Museum of the Smithsonian Institution, is believed to have belonged to John Quincy Adams. Soon after its arrival, the two small leather-bound books on the worktable, the *Oeuvres*

de Gresset, with the simple and distinctive engraved bookplate of JOHN QUINCY ADAMS, were a coincidentally appropriate gift to the White House.

Other noteworthy pieces of furniture in the room are the Empire chest of drawers found in White House storage, the fine little worktable at the foot of the bed, the mirrored dressing chest, mahogany washstand, shaving stand, and the well-carved worktable with unusually bold brass pulls placed against the east wall. This is an excellent example of American Empire craftsmanship and is stamped by the hitherto unrecorded cabinetmaker J. BAIRD, CHERRY STREET, NEW YORK.

Decorative and useful ornaments in the room include a fine small astral lamp of the mid-19th century, a pair of graceful Sheffield candlesticks of the classical period, and a silver luster pitcher of the same date.

WHITE HOUSE COLLECTION

THE EMPIRE GUEST ROOM *on the third floor of the President's House; its American Empire furniture includes a sleigh bed which probably belonged to John Quincy Adams.*

MAHOGANY SHAVING STAND, *of the late Empire period, is of a design not often seen in American furniture. Its marble top turns to face the light.*

THE LINCOLN SITTING ROOM occupies the southeast corner of the second floor of the White House. From about the middle of the 19th century until the renovation of 1902, under the Theodore Roosevelt administration, this small room and the adjoining Lincoln Bedroom were used as offices by the President and his staff. However, the original design of the White House called for a large bedroom, with a connecting sitting or dressing room, in each of the building's four corners.

The furniture in this room is of the late Empire and Victorian periods, complementing the collection of Victorian furniture in the Lincoln Bedroom.

The three side chairs and armchair seen in the photograph (opposite) were most likely purchased during the Lincoln administration and have always been a part of the White House Collection. The side chairs have backs of laminated rosewood, an unusual feature that is apparent in the chair shown at the desk.

An Empire worktable at the right of the sofa is a 1962 gift to the White House. Originally owned by the Lee family of Virginia, it bears the stamp: SAM'L CARTER, CABINET MAKER, 51 BEEKMAN ST., NEW YORK.

The walls have been covered with a green and yellow print, copied from one of the patterns so popular in the 19th century. The striped curtains are of a red Paisley design alternating with green print, which matches the wall hangings.

Engravings and mementos of the Lincoln administration have been placed in this room. Among the collection of 19th-century prints relating to the Capital are color lithographs of public buildings and bird's-eye views of Washington and nearby Georgetown. They illustrate the growth of the Federal City. There are also early engravings of L'Enfant's celebrated city plan.

THE LINCOLN SITTING ROOM *contains furniture and other objects, such as the picture below, from the late Empire and Victorian periods. Many prints of Lincoln and his family were issued during his administration, but this color lithograph published by Thomas Kelly of New York is among the most successful.*

PRESENTED TO THE WHITE HOUSE COLLECTION, 1963

THE TREATY ROOM — Chosen by President Andrew Johnson for his Cabinet Room, this room is one door removed from Lincoln's Cabinet Room (today the Lincoln Bedroom). The room continued to serve as the President's Cabinet Room until the renovation of 1902 removed all the offices to the newly built West Office Wing. Photographs of the latter half of the 19th century show the furnishings of this conference chamber: a great pedestal table with its eight locking drawers, a sofa, bookcase, overmantel mirror, and window cornices decorated with the carved shield of the United States, all purchased during the Grant administration. Carpets and curtains, candelabra and busts were consistent with Victorian decor.

In 1902 the chamber was transformed into a sitting room. The inscription seen below was carved on the new mantelpiece, noting the room's former use and history. The furniture was dispersed at this time; the table removed to a room downstairs, and most of the other furnishings sold. A letter from President Theodore Roosevelt authorized the sale of chairs to the members of the Cabinet for $5 apiece. Secretaries Shaw, Knox, Payne, Moody, Hitchcock, Wilson, and Hay each received the following letter from Col. Theodore A. Bingham:

> Mr. Secretary:
> It gives me great pleasure to send you one of the chairs formerly used by the Cabinet meetings at the White House. This chair was purchased in General Grant's time and has been in use till the present time. Owing to the construction of a separate office building equipped with entirely new furniture, this chair was no longer needed for the purpose for which it was purchased, and is therefore, by permission of the President, sent to you as a souvenir.

The old Cabinet Room has been re-created today as the Treaty Room, with some of the original furniture used when it served the Cabinet. It has now become a waiting or meeting room for the President. A sturdy refuge from areas furnished with more delicate pieces of the early 19th century, the room is papered and curtained in the Victorian manner. The background paper resembles deep-green velvet, while the pattern of the border, which has been used to form relieving panels, is copied precisely from the wallpaper that hung in the room across from Ford's Theatre where President Lincoln died. The curtains are based on models of the Victorian era.

The Treaty Room contains some of its original furnishings: the table, the sofa, the swivel chair, and the clock. Additional pieces, all from the same era, and chiefly from White House storage, are very much at home here. The heart-back Victorian chairs were used in the Family Dining Room in the second half of the 19th century (page 119). The round table with gadrooned border is to be seen in old prints of the Library (page 40). The large crystal chandelier is one of three ordered for the East Room by President Grant in 1873, but removed in the renovation of 1902. The elegant overmantel mirror with its gesso and gilt scroll and flower decoration was used originally on the State Floor.

Several gifts made to the White House in 1962 are now in this room. The desk between the windows belonged to Julia Dent Grant; the andirons and fender were used in the White House during the administration of Zachary Taylor; and the side chairs near the window in the room view have portrait busts of Van Buren and Taylor carved in the crest rails. A Victorian side table and two fine astral lamps were also 1962 gifts.

THIS ROOM WAS FIRST USED FOR MEETINGS OF THE CABINET DURING THE ADMINISTRATION OF PRESIDENT JOHNSON. IT CONTINUED TO BE SO USED UNTIL THE YEAR MCMII HERE THE TREATY OF PEACE WITH SPAIN WAS SIGNED.

© WHITE HOUSE HISTORICAL ASSOCIATION

THE TREATY ROOM, *created in the former Cabinet Room of President Andrew Johnson, is furnished with White House pieces of the Victorian period. The mantel inscription (above), carved in 1902, refers to the treaty ending the Spanish-American War. In this room, President Kennedy signed the Test Ban Treaty, October 7, 1963.*

THE PRESIDENT'S CABINET ROOM *did not change very much in appearance between 1869 and 1901, when this photograph was made. The Cabinet table has again been placed in the room, and the swivel armchair (page 86) at the end of the table was recently returned to the White House. The side chairs were sold to the members of Theodore Roosevelt's Cabinet in 1902; one is today at the Smithsonian Institution.*

ROCOCO-REVIVAL ARMCHAIR, *one of a pair recovered from White House storage, similar to the one in the Healy portrait of Lincoln (page 67). The chairs have been reupholstered in wine-red velvet, popular in the Victorian era.*

On the walls of the Treaty Room have been hung White House paintings of particular interest to the room. A portrait of President Andrew Johnson, who first used the chamber as a Cabinet Room, by E. F. Andrews, hangs on the west wall. A portrait of President Grant, by Henry Ulke, hangs to the right of it. The painting of Lincoln's reception of General Grant (page 39) hangs between the windows.

The Treaty Room was so named because of the many pacts signed within it. Treaties dating from the end of the 19th century hang on every wall.

On the north side hangs a painting of one of the most significant events that occurred in the room—"The Signing of the Peace Protocol," which ended hostilities in the Spanish-American War. With its vista of the President's Park through one of the windows of this room, this painting by Theobald Chartran is particularly suitable to the restoration. It shows President McKinley observing American Secretary of State William Day and French Minister Jules Cambon, who is signing the document.

Also in this room is the Healy painting "The Peacemakers," showing President Lincoln, with Generals Grant and Sherman and Admiral Porter, on board the ship *River Queen* discussing the possibilities of peace before termination of the Civil War.

MARBLE CLOCK, *purchased during the Grant administration, was made in New York by Browne and Spaulding. Its three dials are clock, calendar, and barometer, with a center thermometer that indicates temperature refinements such as 90° for an "ordinary bath."*

THE OLD CABINET TABLE *was brought to the East Room when President Calvin Coolidge signed the ratification of the Kellogg-Briand Peace Pact on January 17, 1929.*

IN THE PRESIDENT'S DINING ROOM *the table is set with Lincoln china. On the hunt board are three pieces from the Biennais service purchased by Andrew Jackson.*

THE PRESIDENT'S DINING ROOM, at the west end of the second floor, has always been part of the President's apartments and formerly served as a bedroom or a sitting room. The lack of a dining room on the second floor, long a pressing need, was solved in 1961 when this room was refurnished in its present style and a pantry and kitchen were installed next door.

The room's wall covering seems particularly appropriate to the President's House; it is a later version of the Zuber wallpaper "Scenic America," of 1834, which hangs in the Diplomatic Reception Room. For this paper, "Scenes of the American Revolution," the firm retained the original background but placed events of the Revolution in the foreground (pages 8 and 122).

This paper and the original "Scenic America" were based on engravings of the 1820's by the artist Engelmann, which are today at the New York Public Library. It is interesting to note that of the six views depicted—Niagara Falls, Natural Bridge, Boston Harbor, West Point, New York Bay, and Lake George—four are scenes of New York. This State, perhaps partly because of its variety of landscape, was particularly admired by Europeans, and one view shows the Hudson, often referred to by 19th-century travelers as "the Rhine of America."

The room, lighted by a late 18th-century chandelier, is furnished with American Federal furniture presented to the White House in 1961 and 1962. A Maryland side table, possibly by John Shaw of Annapolis, the handsome hunt board of Southern origin, the New England sideboard which belonged to Daniel Webster, and the small caned settee are among the excellent examples included in this chamber. Rectangular-back side chairs are placed around the pedestal table, and the colors used in the room are based on the scenic wallpaper. The blue silk window hangings follow a pattern in a design book of the early 19th century.

THIS MAHOGANY SIDEBOARD *with inlaid eagle has an unusual pull-out desk section. Its history and the initials D. W. in the inner case attest to its ownership by Daniel Webster.*

PRESENTED TO THE WHITE HOUSE COLLECTION, 1962

THE PRESIDENT'S OFFICE *in the West Wing. Behind the desk stand the American flag and the Presidential flag, bearing the Seal of the Chief Executive.*

THE PRESIDENT'S OFFICE—In 1902 the enlargement and renovation sought by a succession of 19th-century Presidents became a reality. President Theodore Roosevelt requested funds for this purpose, and the Civil Appropriation Act of June, 1902, provided for "a building to accommodate the offices of the President, to be located in the grounds of the Executive Mansion. . . ."

The building of the West Office Wing solved a twofold problem: It removed from the house proper the crowded and sometimes noisy offices and conference chambers, and, consequently, allowed an expansion of the President's private apartments in the space thus freed. The building erected at this time by McKim, Mead & White was considered a temporary structure because general agreement could not be reached on a permanent location. However, the President's present oval office was added to the wing in 1909, and the structure has continued in use until today.

The West Wing, in scale and decoration, and joined to the house as it is by the rebuilt Jefferson pavilion, is in perfect harmony with the original building. Indeed, the sensitivity of President Roosevelt and the architects to the original character and plan of the mansion is the most notable feature of the renovation. The firm stated in its report to the President of February, 1903, at the completion of its work, that it had adhered wholeheartedly to his request that "the nation's historic house should be left intact, and that even the state rooms should continue to be known by the names made familiar by long usage. . . ."

The office, oval in form, repeats the most interesting architectural feature of the President's House—Hoban's "elliptic saloon." Admirably proportioned and filled with natural light, it looks out on a traditional American garden, the Rose Garden.

The office is furnished with both White House furniture and personal possessions of the President. A portrait of Washington by Gilbert Stuart, based on the artist's unfinished life portrait of the first President, dominates the room from its position over the mantel. At the left of the President's desk hangs G. P. A. Healy's study of Henry Clay, while a portrait of Andrew Jackson by Thomas Sully hangs at the right.

THE EXTERIOR OF THE PRESIDENT'S OFFICE: *French doors open on a colonnade, similar to and adjoining Jefferson's pavilion. The colonnade faces the Rose Garden, bordered with boxwood and holly osmanthus.*

THE CABINET ROOM *in the West Wing. Like the President's Office, this room faces the Rose Garden. A portrait of Thomas Jefferson by Matthew H. Jouett hangs over the mantelpiece; the Cabinet table was presented during the administration of Franklin Roosevelt. From 1865 until the renovation of the White House in 1902, the Cabinet met on the second floor of the mansion in an Executive Office today known as the Treaty Room (page 140).*

THE CABINET ROOM, in the West Wing of the White House, is, except for the President's Office itself, the scene of more historic decisions than any other room in the contemporary White House. Here, in a light and pleasant room, looking out on the Rose Garden, the Cabinet meets; here also the National Security Council holds its sessions; here the President talks with legislative leaders or with other groups too large for his own office. The Cabinet Room is separated from the President's Office by the office of his personal secretary.

Before the construction of the West Wing in 1902, by the architectural firm of McKim, Mead & White, it was customary for the President to meet with the Cabinet in the Executive Offices located on the second floor of the White House. The room designated for such meetings from 1865 through 1902 can be seen in the photograph which appears on page 140. Known as the Treaty Room today, it is furnished with several of the Victorian pieces used by the President and Cabinet members during the last century.

A portrait of Thomas Jefferson by Matthew H. Jouett hangs above the mantel (opposite). It is a 19th-century copy of the Gilbert Stuart life portrait of our third President. The painting faces two others of leading Americans: a portrait of Andrew Jackson in military uniform by Ralph Earl (on loan from the Smithsonian Institution), and a portrait of Daniel Webster attributed to artist Bass Otis. A copy of the famous portrait of Franklin D. Roosevelt by the noted English portraitist Frank O. Salisbury hangs in the center of the west wall.

On the mantel, below the portrait of Jefferson, is a clock that was formerly aboard the U.S.S. *Williamsburg,* the Presi-

PRESENTED TO THE WHITE HOUSE COLLECTION, 1962

DANIEL WEBSTER'S PORTRAIT *is attributed to Bass Otis. Webster served as Secretary of State for three Presidents between 1840-1853.*

dential yacht during the Truman administration.

This long, windowed conference chamber is simply furnished with a massive and dignified table presented to the White House in Franklin Roosevelt's administration by Secretary of Commerce Jesse H. Jones, and with comfortable leather-covered armchairs, each with the appropriate Cabinet member's title inscribed on the back.

The room, which faces the Rose Garden, is lined with bookshelves on the west wall; the flag of the United States and the Presidential flag flank the Great Seal recessed in the east wall. The President's chair is at right center of the table.

FORMERLY ABOARD *the U.S.S.* Williamsburg *this clock, with its matching barometer, now rests on the Cabinet Room mantel. The* Williamsburg *served as Presidential yacht in the Truman administration.*

THE GARDENS — The first White House garden was planned for John Adams. In a diary entry of March 20, 1800, a Washingtonian wrote: "After breakfast we walked ... to the ground behind the President's House, which [will be] enclosed and laid out for a garden. It is at present in great confusion, having on it old brick kilns, pits to contain Water used by the brick makers. . . ." The type of garden thus planned is not known, for the writer did not elaborate.

The Rose Garden, which adjoins the President's Office, was first planted with roses in 1913 by the first Mrs. Woodrow Wilson. Except for rearrangements resulting from the enlargement of the Executive Office in 1936 and from the renovation of the mansion in 1952, no significant changes were made in the Rose Garden until 1962.

President Kennedy then called upon Mrs. Paul Mellon to redesign the garden and to provide space to receive public groups.

The resulting plan was that of a traditional 18th-century American garden. Planting beds form the long lines of the rectangle framed by holly osmanthus and boxwood hedges, while five flowering crab apples are placed at intervals in each bed.

The spring flowers include tulip, crocus, narcissus, and other bulb plants. Before these fade they are replaced by pansies, Shasta daisies, geraniums, columbines, and other favorites. In the fall, chrysanthemums, salvia, and heliotrope bloom in profusion. When frost ends the chrysanthemums, foliage replaces the bright plantings.

Thousands of visitors have been welcomed to the White House in the Rose

IN THE FALL, *chrysanthemums fill the beds of the Jacqueline Kennedy Garden. In the background, at the west end of the garden, is an arbor paved with handmade brick.*

IN MIDSUMMER, *the Rose Garden is filled with annuals and perennials: roses, heliotrope, geraniums, lilies, and nicotiana. The President's Office overlooks the garden from the West Wing, which is shaded by magnolia trees.*

Garden. Among groups greeted by the President have been Medal of Honor recipients, America's first team of astronauts, and many foreign delegations. The garden has also served as the setting for a state dinner.

Designated by President and Mrs. Lyndon B. Johnson as the Jacqueline Kennedy Garden, the former East Garden has a somewhat obscure history. During the 19th century it was primarily a lawn area with flowering beds, shrubs, and ornamental trees. The first plan for the garden is attributed to Mrs. Theodore Roosevelt. Additional changes were made in 1913 and 1952.

The Jacqueline Kennedy Garden is intended primarily for the use of the First Lady, her family, and friends. Its present restoration, begun while the late President Kennedy was in office, reflects the phi-losophy of Washington and Jefferson, who believed that a garden must have reason as well as being decorative.

As in the Rose Garden, two large *Magnolia soulangeana alexandrina* have been planted in the northwest and southwest corners. Other trees include a row of lindens which form an aerial hedge against the building and provide shade for the glassed-in colonnade. The east end of the garden is planted with hollies, magnolias, and crab apples. In the center of each square planting bed are clipped American hollies which are surrounded by spring bulbs and annuals that are changed with the seasons.

The west end of the garden features an arbor with a surface of handmade brick, and a shallow pool has been placed at the east end.

I Pray Heaven To Bestow
THE BEST OF BLESSINGS ON

From a Letter of
JOHN ADAMS

This House

November
MDCCC

And All that shall hereafter Inhabit it
May none but Honest and Wise Men ever rule
under This Roof.

THE PRESIDENTS

GEORGE WASHINGTON	*April 30, 1789 — March 3, 1797*
JOHN ADAMS	*March 4, 1797 — March 3, 1801*
THOMAS JEFFERSON	*March 4, 1801 — March 3, 1809*
JAMES MADISON	*March 4, 1809 — March 3, 1817*
JAMES MONROE	*March 4, 1817 — March 3, 1825*
JOHN QUINCY ADAMS	*March 4, 1825 — March 3, 1829*
ANDREW JACKSON	*March 4, 1829 — March 3, 1837*
MARTIN VAN BUREN	*March 4, 1837 — March 3, 1841*
WILLIAM HENRY HARRISON	*March 4, 1841 — April 4, 1841*
JOHN TYLER	*April 6, 1841 — March 3, 1845*
JAMES K. POLK	*March 4, 1845 — March 3, 1849*
ZACHARY TAYLOR	*March 5, 1849 — July 9, 1850*
MILLARD FILLMORE	*July 10, 1850 — March 3, 1853*
FRANKLIN PIERCE	*March 4, 1853 — March 3, 1857*
JAMES BUCHANAN	*March 4, 1857 — March 3, 1861*
ABRAHAM LINCOLN	*March 4, 1861 — April 15, 1865*
ANDREW JOHNSON	*April 15, 1865 — March 3, 1869*
ULYSSES S. GRANT	*March 4, 1869 — March 3, 1877*
RUTHERFORD B. HAYES	*March 3, 1877 — March 3, 1881*
JAMES A. GARFIELD	*March 4, 1881 — September 19, 1881*
CHESTER A. ARTHUR	*September 20, 1881 — March 3, 1885*
GROVER CLEVELAND	*March 4, 1885 — March 3, 1889*
BENJAMIN HARRISON	*March 4, 1889 — March 3, 1893*
GROVER CLEVELAND	*March 4, 1893 — March 3, 1897*
WILLIAM MCKINLEY	*March 4, 1897 — September 14, 1901*
THEODORE ROOSEVELT	*September 14, 1901 — March 3, 1909*
WILLIAM H. TAFT	*March 4, 1909 — March 3, 1913*
WOODROW WILSON	*March 4, 1913 — March 3, 1921*
WARREN G. HARDING	*March 4, 1921 — August 2, 1923*
CALVIN COOLIDGE	*August 3, 1923 — March 3, 1929*
HERBERT HOOVER	*March 4, 1929 — March 3, 1933*
FRANKLIN D. ROOSEVELT	*March 4, 1933 — April 12, 1945*
HARRY S TRUMAN	*April 12, 1945 — January 20, 1953*
DWIGHT D. EISENHOWER	*January 20, 1953 — January 20, 1961*
JOHN F. KENNEDY	*January 20, 1961 — November 22, 1963*
LYNDON B. JOHNSON	*November 22, 1963 —*

LYNDON B. JOHNSON, *the present Chief Executive of the United States.*

THE PRESIDENT'S PARK — *This drawing is based on an aerial photograph and a plan drawn by the National Park Service. The trees and other landscape features shown in darker green are associated with Presidents and are identified in the key at right.*

O

W

T

P

X

M

J

A

E

E

H

SOUTH EXECUTIVE AVE.